THE PLAN

AFTER POLICE REFORM That Will _Guarantee_ Social Justice & Progress for the Black Community

Reco M. McCambry, MBA

Contact the author or publisher if you would like information about how to access any and all programs or other materials associated with this book and its contents.

This book may be purchased for educational, business, sales, or promotional use. For information or to order, please contact:

Email: info@ThePlanAfterReform.com
Website: www.ThePlanAfterReform.com

Office: (678) 379-7211
Fax: (678) 528-9513

1257B Commercial Dr SW
Conyers, GA 30094

Disclaimer

This publication is designed to educate and provide general information regarding the subject matter covered. However, laws and practices often vary from state to state and are subject to change.

Because each factual situation is different, specific advice should be tailored to particular circumstances. For this reason, the reader is advised to consult with his or her own advisor regarding that individual's specific situation.

The author has taken reasonable precautions in the preparation of this book and believes the facts presented in the book are accurate as of the date it was written. However, neither the author nor the publisher assume any responsibility for any errors or omissions.

The author and publisher specifically disclaim any liability resulting from the use or application of the information contained in this book, and the information is not intended to serve as legal advice related to individual situations.

Table of Contents

Dedication

This book is dedicated to the thousands of Black people who have lost their lives to police violence, suspicious deaths ruled suicides, and other means that involved racial injustice, and their families.

In recognition of the names I could find and to display the magnitude of this horrific reality, this book is dedicated especially to the memories and families of:

George Floyd – Breonna Taylor – Trayvon Martin – Ahmaud Arbery – Eric Garner – John Crawford III – Michael Brown – Ezell Ford – Dante Parker – Michelle Cusseaux – Laquan McDonald – George Mann – Tanisha Anderson – Akai Gurley – Tamir Rice – Rumain Brisbon – Jerame Reid – Matthe Ajibade – Frank Smart – Natasha McKenna – Tony Robinson Phillip White – Eric Harris – Walter Scott – William Chapman II – Alexia Christian – Brendon Glen – Victor Manuel Larosa – Jonathan Sanders – Freddie Gray – Leslie Sapp III – Ron Sneed – Hashim Hanif Ibn Abdul-Rasheed – Omarr Julian Maximillian Jackson – Artago Damon Howard – Marcus Golden – Mario Jordan – Donte Sowell – Kavonda Earl Payton – Terence Walker – Dewayne Carr – Isaac Holmes – Tiano Meton – Demaris Turner – Darin Hutchins – Jermonte Fletcher – Edward Donnell Bright – Ledarius D. Williams – Yuvette Henderson – Dewayne Deshawn Ward – Jeremy Lett – Jimmy Ray Robinson Jr. – Markell Atkins – Herbert Hill – James Allen – Desmond Luster – Anthony Bess – Phillip Watkins – Lavall Hall – Janisha Fonville – Stanley Lamar Grant – Douglas Harris – A'Donte Washington – Glenn Lewis – Thomas Allen – Cornelius J. Parker – Ian Sherrod – Charly Leundeu Keunang – Shaquille Barrow – Fednel Rhinvil – Tyrone Ryerson Lawrence – Sandra Bland – Naeschylus Vinzant – Andrew Anthony Williams – Monique Jenee Deckard – Anthony Hill – Cedrick Lamont Bishop – Theodore Johnson – Jamie Croom – Terry

Garnett Jr. – Bobby Gross – Brandon Jones – Kendre Alston – Richard White – Denzel Brown – Devin Gates – Walter J. Brown III – Nicholas Thomas – Jeremy Lorenza Kelly – Megan Hockaday – Angelo West – Jamalis Hall – Byron Herbert – Mya Hall – Robert Washington – Darrin Langford – Justus Howell – Paul Anderson – Desmond Willis – Dexter Pernell Bethea – Don Smith – Mack Long – Coby Robinson – Tevin Barkley – Dante Noble – Frank Shephard – Jeffrey Kemp – Thaddeus McCarroll – Daniel Wolfe – William Chapman – Reginald McGregor – Todd Jamal Dye – David Felix – Terrance Kellom – Jared Johnson – Jeffrey Adkins – Elton Simpson – Brendon Glenn – Nephi Arriguin – Dedrick Marshall – Sam Holmes – Lionel Lorenzo Young – Kelvin Goldston – D'Angelo Stallworth – Ronell Wade – Anthony Gomez – Chrislon Talbott – Marcus Wheeler – Javoris Washington – Jerome Caldwell – Caso Jackson – Anthony Briggs – Dalton Branch – James Strong – Kenneth Dothard – Kevin Allen – Usaamah Rahim – Demouria Hogg – QuanDavier Hicks – Isiah Hampton – Charles Ziegler – Fritz Severe – Deng Manyoun – Kris Jackson – Trepierre Hummons – Alfontish Cockerham – Tyrone Harris – Damien A. Harrel – Spencer McCain – Kevni Lamont Judson – Victor Emanuel Larosa – Robert Elando Malone – Kawanza Beaty – Jason Hendley – Marcellus Jamarcus Burley – Tremaine Dantzler – Martice Milliner – Javon Hawkins – Freddie Blue – Eugene McSwain – Salvado Ellswood – Frederick Farmer – Chacarion Avant – Edward Foster III – Anthonie Smith – Albert Joseph Davis – Darrius Stewart – Billy Ray Davis – Samuel DuBose – Michael Sabbie – Brian Keith Day – Christian Taylor – Troy Robinson – Devon Guisherd – Andre Dontrell Williams – Dontae L. Martin – Bryan Keith Day – Earl Jackson – Khari Westly – Antonio Clements – Darius D. Graves – Raymond Hodge – Keshawn Dominique Hargrove – Charles Bertram – Christian Taylor – Tsombe Clark – Derrick Lee Hunt – Shamir Terrel Palmer – Andre Green – Nathaniel Wilks – Reginald Marshall – Redel Jones – Garland Tyree – Asshams Pharoah Manley – Allen Matthew Baker – Benjamin Peter

Ashley – Frederick Roy – Mansur Ball-Bey – Deviere Ernel Ransom
– Thaddeus Faison – Bobby Troledge Norris – Curtis Smith – Yonas
Alehegne – Bertrand Davis – Felix Kumi – James Marcus Brown –
Cedric Maurice Williams – La'vante Trevon Biggs – Angelo Delano
Perry – Mohamed Ibrahim – Tyrone Holman – Brandon Foy –
Clifford Butler – Joseph Thompson Johnson-Shanks – Tyrone Bass –
Bobby R. Anderson – Dante Osborne – Keith Harrison McLeod –
Jeremy McDole – Anthony McKinney – James Anderson – Junior
Prosper – Brandon Lamar Johnson – Jeffery McCallum – Charles A.
Pettit – Gary Carmona Boitano – Bernard Brandon Powers – Jason
Day – Leslie Portis – Kaleb Alexander – Martin Ryans Jr. – Ricky
Javenta Ball – Dequan Williams – Corey Jones – Dion Lamont
Ramirez – Lamontez Jones – Paterson Brown – Lawrence Green –
Adriene Jamarr Ludd – Rolly Thomas – Dominic Hutchinson – Kevin
Brunson – Marquesha McMillan – Tyrie Cuyler – Anthony Ashford –
Alonzo Smith – Tyree Crawford – India Kager – La'Vante Biggs –
Michael Lee Marshall – Jerry Michael Graham Jr. – Deaunte Lamar
Bell – Tony Berry – Brian Crawford – James Covington – John Allen
– Delvin Simmons – Ryan Quinn Martin – Moises Nero – Shane
Whitehead – Jamar Clark – Richard Perkins – Nathaniel Harris
Pickett – Bennie Lee Tignor – Yohans Leon – Demetrius Bryant –
Jeray Chatham – Cornelius Brown – Marcus Meridy – Randy Allen
Smith – Steve Dormil – Darick Napper – Freddy Baez – Darius Smith
– Mario Woods – Raymone M. Davis – Carlumandarlo Zaramo –
Miguel Espinal – Derek Stokes – Charles Edward Rosemond –
Christopher Goodlow – Javario Shante Eagle – Nicholas Robertson –
Calvin McKinnis – Ronnie Dubose Carter – Trayvon Scruggs – Leroy
Browning – Bobby Daniels – Michael Noel – Chan Leith – Kevin
Matthews – Terrozza Tyree Griffin – Bettie Jones – Quintonio Legrier
– Keith Childress Jr. – Janet Wilson – Randy Nelson – Germonta
Wallace – Eric John Senegal – Rodney Turner – Carlton Antonio
Murphy – Rakeem Bentley – Henry Bennett – Crayton West –
Timothy Albert – Cedrin Norris – Johnathan Bratcher – Christopher

Kalonji – Randolph McClain – Christopher Michael Dew – Charles M. Smith – Bruce Kelley – Peter John – Antronie Scott – Wendell Celestine – Marese V. Collins – Shalamar Longer – David Joseph – Eric Harris – Mohamed Barry – Peter Fanfan – Sahlah Ridgeway – Calvin Smith – Calin Roquemore – Dyzhawn L. Perkins – Marco Loud – Peter Gaines – Torrey Robinson – Darius Robinson – Ali Eisa Abdalla Yahia – Paul Gaston – Marcos Perea – Che Taylor – Kisha Michael – Travis Stevenson – Marquintan Sandlin – Christopher J. Davis – Greg Gunn – Cedric Ford – Kionte Desean Spencer – Akiel Denkins – Arteair Porter Jr. – Tyre Privott – Keith Montgomery Jr. – Jacai Colson – Lamar Harris – Scott Bennett – Christopher Nelms – India Beaty – Thurman Reynolds – Robert Dentmond – Alexio Allen – Dominique Silva – Jermon Seals – Deriante Deon Miller – Kimani Johnson – Matthew Vincent Wood – James Brown III – James Craig Simpson – Cameron Gover – Kevin Hicks – Mary Truxillo – Terrill Thomas – Laronda Sweatt – Dazion Flenaugh – Lamont Gulley – Diahlo Grant – Quron Williams – Pierre Loury – Rodney Watts – Kisha Arrone – Richard Bard Jr. – George Tillman – Edson Thevenin – Rico Don Rae Johnson – Demetrius Dorsey – Jorevis Scruggs – Demarcus Semer – Willie Tillman – Joshua Brooks – Kendar del Rosario – Ashtian Barnes – Charlin Charles – Reginald Darnell Dogan – Burt Johnson – Deresha Armstrong – Ronald D. Williams – Alton Fitzgerald Witchard – Lionel Gibson – Jaffort Smith – Arthur R. Williams – Arthur DaRosa – Sean Ryan Mondragon – Jabril Robinson – Jessica Nelson-Williams – Kentrill William Carraway – Joshua Beebee – Michael Eugene Wilson Jr. – Vernell Bing – Doll Pierre-Louis – Devonte Gates – Dennis Hudson – Osee Calix – Michael Johnson – Willie Demetrius James – Rodney Rodriguez Smith – Demarco Rhymes – Henry Green – Willis N. Walker – John Michael Brisco – Keith Bursey – Lyndarius Cortez Witherspoon – John Williams – Michael Moore – Antwun Shumpert – Rashaun Lloyd – Raufeal M. Bostick – Isaiah Core – Quencezola Maurice Splunge – Deravis Caine Rogers – Jay Anderson – Angelo Brown –

Ismael Miranda – Germichael Kennedy – Donte L. Johnson –
Sherman Evans – Tyrone Reado – Lafayette Evans – Kawme Dejuan
Patrick – Jai Lateef Solveig Williams – Sidney Washington – Alton
Sterling – Philando Castile – Terence Crutcher – Earnest Fells –
Andre Johnson – Alva Burnett Braziel – Joseph Mann – Jason Brooks
– Orville Edwards – Dayten Ernest Harper – Jermaine Johnson –
Gavin Eugene Long – Derek Love – Austin Jerry Lee Howard –
Bernard Wells – Jeff Cornell Tyson – Richard Risher – Devon Martes
– Dalvin Hollins – Jeffrey Smith – Paul O'Neal – Donnell Thompson
– Korryn Gaines – DeMarco Newman – Jamarion Rashad Robinson –
Jawari Porter – Earl Pinckney – Darnell Wicker – Syville Smith –
Colby Friday – Kenney Watkins – Omer Ismail Ali – Kelley Brandon
Forte – Donta Taylor – Jaqwan Julius Terry – Levonia Riggins –
Michael Thompson – Jerome Damon – Moses Ruben – Robert Lee
Brown – Sadiq Bishara-Abaker Idris – Gregory Frazier – Terrence
Sterling – Markell Bivins – Tyre King – Terence Crutcher – Nicholas
Glenn – Philip Hasan – Keith Lamont Scott – Oddis Bernard Colvin –
Alfred Olango – Christopher Sowell – George Richards-Meyers –
Douglas Marrickus Rainey – Najier Salaam – Jacquarius M.
Robinson – Carnell Snell – Donte T. Jones – Larry Daniel Matthews –
Christopher Darnell Shackleford – Deric J. Brown – Kirk Figueroa –
Darius Wimberly – Deborah Danner – Demetrius Mac Moore –
Aaron Marquis Ballard – Roy Lee Richards – Malcolm Loren
Hickson – Thad Demarco Hale – Jason King – Terrence Coleman –
Michelle Lee Shirley – Ferguson Laurent – Darryl Chisholm –
Andrew Depeiza – Rasheem Singletary – Dontrell Montrese Carter –
Darius Jones – Samson Fleurant – Erickson Brito – George Bush III –
Ivory C. Pantallion – Frank Nathaniel Clark – Talif Scudder – Kajuan
Raye – Cleotha Mitchell – Jerome Chris Harmon – Richard Grimes –
Terrell Walker – Irecas Valentine – David K. Crosby-Dowdy – Bruce
Randall "Zeus" Johnson – Norman Gary – Redrick Jevon Batiste –
Mark Anthony Hicks – Waltki Williams – Kenneth Robledo – Lavar
Montray Douglas – Earl Labon Eubanks – Ryan Joseph – Anthony

Lovell Eddington – Terrence Thomas – Daquan Antonio Westbrook – Gerald Hall – Jamal Rollins – Trevon Johnson – Mark Guirguis – James E. Lewis – James Owens – Ruben Randolph – Jamal Parks – J.R. Williams – Davion Henderson – Darrion Barnhill – Jahlire Nicholson – Herbert Johnson – Marquis Thomas – Ronnie Lee Shorter – Christopher Thompkins – Armond Brown – Arties Manning – Kevin Darnell Washington – Deaundre Phillips – Mi'Chance Dunlap-Gittens – Marvin Washington – Tavis Crane – Michael Russo – Jamake Cason Thomas – Johnnie J. Harris – Nana Adomako – Shelly Porter – Jerome Allen – Cole Wooley – Curtis Jamal Deal – Chad Robertson – Quanice Derrick Hayes – Jocques Scott Clemmons – Carlos Keith Blackman – Darryl L. Fuqua – Alonzo E. Ashley – Willard Eugene Scott – Raynard Burton – Kenneth Lee Bailey – Kadeem Torres – Jimmy Briggs – Jean R. Valescot – Chance David Baker – Keo Crockett – Christopher Carter – Don Clark – Medger Blake – Morgan London Rankins – Timothy Lionel Williams – Lorenzo Antione Cruz – Earl Riley – Christopher Redding – Epthen Lamont Johnson – Dennis Todd Rogers – Brandon Wiley – Luke O. Stewart – Rashad Daquan Opher – Cordale Quinn Handy – Frederick Ricardo Brown – Jermaine Claybrooks – Rodney James Hess – Patrick Earl Gatson – Desmond Phillips – Alteria Woods – Don Johnson – William Stokes – Eddie Davis – Reno Joseph Owens – Leroy Brown – Marcus Williams – Christopher Wade – Richard Xavier Summers – Kenneth Francis – Zelalem Eshetu Ewnetu – Olugbalah Ridley – Keith Price – Damarius Butts – William D. Spates – Kendell Wilson – Daezion Turner – Hakim McNair – Gavin Williams – Selwyn Aubrey Hall – Burgon Sealy – Avery Richard – Jordan Edwards – Caleb Jackson – James Edward Ray – Rodney Henderson – Malik Carey – Cedric Jamal Mifflin – Landon Nobles – Mikel Laney McIntyre – Terry Percy Campbell – Terrell Kyreem Johnson – Robin White – Ronald Singletary – Clarence E. Coats – Jonie Block – Jaison Fitzgerald – Tristan Long – Jimmie Montel Sanders – Ricco Devante Holden – Shaquian Tyrone Johnson –

Charles Darnell Baker – Marc Brandon Davis – Corsean Lewis – John Spaulding – Adrian Maurice Hardeman – David Jones – Joshua Barre – Terry Williams – Jordan Frazier – Chazz Brown – Charleena Lyles – Giovonn Joseph-McDade – Lawrence Heyward Jr. – Deveonte Johnson – Rodney L. Cole – Aaron Baily – Joel Gatu Muturi – Quintec Locke – Dana Dubose – Zepp Crouchet – Alexander Bonds – Dejuan Guillory – Brian Easely – Kareem Ali Nadir Jones – Cardell Vance III – Edward Taylor – Antonio Garcia Jr. – Vaughn Shaw – India N. Nelson – Isaiah Perkins – Aries Clark – Kesharn K. Burney – Deltra Henderson – Rodney E. Jacobs – Jashod Arthur Carter – Dwayne Jeune – Isaiah Tucker – Kerry Bradley – Preston Thornton – Quintas Harris – Kemonte Cobbs – Danatae Franklin – Darreon Neal – Eugene Nelson – Tyrease Carlyle – Patrick Harmon – Hussein Hassan – Herbert Gilbert – Kenneth Lewis – Derrick Rashard Brabham – Keshawn Wilson – Nathaniel Richmond – Kiwi Herring – Scott Mayfield – Charles David Robinson – Michael Malik Kawon Lee – William Matthew Holmes – Ricky Ard – Anthony Antonio Ford – Antwon Springer – Jarvis Hayes – Miguel Richards – Eric Dwan Arnold – Ervin Eugene Sweat Jr. – Brian Ziro – Eddie Russell Jr. – Haraesheo Rice – Damien Murray – Anthony Robinson – Demilo Trayuon Hodge – Tyrell Dewayne Pinkston – Marquis "Bubba" Jones – Sandy Guardiola – Jomekia Minter – Corey Boykin – Cariann Hithon – John Robert Payne – J. C. Hawkins – Eric Garrison – DeAndre Bethea – Dewboy Lister – Jamarco McShann – Timothy Earl Jackson – Antonio Levison – Jerry Richardson – Eric Higgs – Kalin Jackson – Luvelle Kennon – Vincent Hall – Raymond Davis – Augustus Joshua Crawford – Eddie Lee Patterson – Jarrett Varnado – Paul Jones – Thomas Aikens – John Bazemore III – Phillip Pitts – Cornell Lockhart – Calvin Toney – Chester Randolph Ward – Shady Bell – Lawrence Hawkins – Rehyen Bost-McMurray – Jackie Germaine Ragland – Aquoness Cathery – Rufus Cedric Baker – Keita O'Neil – Johnnie D. Carter – Jean Pedro Pierre – Frederick Douglas Wilburn – Zoe Dowdell – Michael Wilson – Todd A. Stone – Jesse

Scarsbrook – Dennis Plowden – Corey Bailey – Shaleem Tindle – Ledarren D. Mixon – Charles Smith Jr. – John Bailon – Trayvon Mitchell – Richard R. Towler – Travis Griffin – Shalun Dique Smith – Jonathan Bennett – Terry Amons – Amanuel Dagebo – Geraldine Townsend – Jihad Merrick – Brian Gregory – Donte D. Shannon – Kevin Sturgis – Arther McAfee Jr. – Ricky Jerome Boyd – Corey Mobley – Nathaniel T. Edwards – William Pollard – Crystalline Barnes – Billy Lewis Rucker – Michael Hansford – Albert E. Morton – Daniel O. El – Anthony Joe Williams – Brett Dontae Bush – Mitchell Kitchen – Anthony Jacob Weber – Tierre Guthrie – David Darden – Sidney T. Richardson – Mark Daniels – Ronnell Foster – Jimmy Terry – Lamar Green – Lawrence Shaw – Glenn Tyndell – Lonnie Smith – Edward Hallinan – Lee Edward Bonner – Darion Baker – Joshua D. Babb – Mario Dantonio Bass – Haydon Taylor – William Watson – Marlon Smith – Qawi A. Muhammad – Timothy M. Gray – James Vaughn – Marvin McMillian – James E. Waters – Jamil Harvey – Daniel Stacey Reynolds – Decynthia Clements – Michael Ward – Jontell Reedom – Schermichael Ezeff – Cameron Hall – James Alfonso Vaughn – Stephon Clark – Antwon Rose – Botham Jean – Pamela Turner – Dominique Clayton – Atatiana Jefferson – Christopher Whitfield – Christopher McCorvey – Eric Reason – Jermaine Massey – Danny Thomas – Linus F. Phillip – Rodney Toler – Edward Van McCrae – Bobby Hinton – Timothy Wyatt – Brian Bellamy – Christopher Hall – Deshawn Antonio Carswell – Saheed Vassell – Terrance Eppenger – Diante Yarber – Juan Markee Jones – Elijah James Smith – Grechario Mack – Kenneth Ross – Dashaun Shepard – Rumondale Jones – Steven Brooks – Andre Lavance Rippy – Lonnie Marcel Bowen – Sanchez Lowe – Dytadious Mobley – David Teneyuque – James Bauduy – Terrence Carlton – Demonjhea Jordan – Isaac Jackson – Carlos Deone High – Abadi Gebregziber – Timothy Raye Mayfield – Damion Collier – Terence Leslie – Elliott Reed – Willie Rogers Marable – Anthony Trice – Marcus-David L. Peters – Ronald Clinton

– Juvan Simon – Jerick Rasheem Gray – Gus Tousis – Maurice
Granton – Raymon Truitt – LaShanda Anderson – Robert Lawrence
White – DeNathe M. Guilliford – Marqueese Alston – Chavius Hollis
– Terrence White – Timothy Mosley – Dwayne Clyburn – Tahaji
Wells – Jonathan Buckley – Anthony Marcell Green – Timothy Deal
– Thurman Blevins – Detandel Pickens Devon – Rodney Lee Hunter
– Chukwumankpam Mbegbu – Lemuel Bunn – Terrel Eason –
Charles Webb – Rashaun Washington – Harith Augustus – Jethro
Benjamin – Marlin Mack – Devaughdre Delsha Rogers – DMario
Perkins – Daniel Hambrick – Cynthia Fields – Lamar C. Richardson –
James Edward Blackmon – David Edward Hall – Tramaine Marquese
Poole – Danny Lee – Spurgeon Daniels – Levester Taylor – Ricardo
Giddings – Vaughn Denham – Stephen L. Caldwell – Charles
Meadows – Gregory Campfield – Montae Shackleford – Anthony
Makai Hutchinson – Christopher Anthony Stone – Mario Hobson –
Adrian Herron – Aquantis Givens – Christopher Alexander Okamoto
– Jeremiah Perdue – Jeffrey Dennis – James Clay – Jalon Johnson –
Oshae Terry – Aaron Demonta Fleming – James Leatherwood –
Darell Richards – DaShawn Cole – Brandon Joyner – Dereshia
Blackwell – Thomas Watkins – Detric Driver – Jerry Foster –
Nathaniel Sassafras – Dravious Burch – Paul Braswell – Datwan
Keyo Lewis – Patrick K. Kimmons – LaJuana Philips – Toby Bailey –
Sershawn Martez Dillon – Terrell Blake – Alonzo L. Smith –
Diamonte Riviore – Samuel Morris – Eric Jamar Lupain Stromer –
Keyshon Parham – Charles Roundtree – Jacob Servais – Mahlon
Edward Summerour – Neico Crooks, Jr. – Cedric Pritchard – Tafahree
Maynard – Armond Beckwith-Bell – Christopher Carroll – Albert
Ramon Dorsey – Derrick Alexander Sellman – Tony Bernard Smith –
Jesse J. Quinton – Laudemer Arboleda – Theoddeus Gray – Travis
Jordan – Patrick Bryant – Jemel Roberson – Tony Mathis – Timothy
Leon – Olajuwon Murphy – Allen Fanning – Jack Fields, Jr. – Rio
Antwuan Thomas – Roderick McDaniel – Eugene Benjamin Weathers
– Emantic Fitzgerald Bradford – Martez Webb – Jarmane Logan –

John Young – Jarvis Randall – Demontry Floytra Boyd – Anthony M. Edwards – Dimaggio McNelly – Julius Ervin Tate – Joshua Boyd – Christopher Deandre Mitchell – Marcus Neal – Tameka LeShay Simpson – Demario Bass – Andre Horton – April Webster – Angel Viola Decarlo – Danny Washington – Michael Jerome Taylor – Wayne Falana – Shane Lyons – Kerry D. Blake – Brandon Lovell Webster – Matthew Burroughs – Abdoulaye Thiam – Jae Wesley Hardy – Zonell Williams – Lawrence Thompson III – Kevin Shawn Hanson – Andre C. Gladen – Johnny Lee Burney – Juston Landry – Treshun Symone Miller – Jacob Michael Harris – Jahmal Derrick Stewart – Nathaniel Holland – William Owens – D'ettrick Griffin – Quency Chavez Floyd – D'Angelo Brown – Mikyas Mehary Tegegne – Jimmy Atchison – Dwight Steward – Gregory Griffin – Nekiylo Dawayne Graves – Johnny Weeks – Isaiah Thomas – Corey Johnson – Anthony Dewayne Childs – Allon Jones – Bruce Carter – Willie Bo McCoy – Willie Jermaine Robinson – Ty'rell Pounds – Alex Johnson – Christopher Brimsey – Patrick Reed – Gary Marin – Michael Elam – Reginald Romero Bursey – Pierre Woods – Emanuel David Joshua Oates – Kyron Marcell Sands – Bradley Blackshire – Neico Crooks – James Scott Reed – Luke Anthony Swann – Shamikle Jackson – Antonio Joseph Valentine – Donqaule Maurice Gray – Rodney Lassiter – Latasha Nicole Walton – Charles Ballard – Nina Adams – Thomas Johnson – Osaze Osagie – Daishawn Brown – Derek Smith – Kevin Bruce Mason – Danquirs Napoleon Franklin – Kaylon Robinson – Chris Joseph – Daviri Robertson – Brian Leslie Statler – Pierre J. Cher Frere – Ondrae Levado Hutchinson – Oscar Cain – Veltavious Griggs – Bishar Hassan – Anthony Orlando Bowers – Marzeus Scott – Harold Vincent Robinson – Terry Davis – Trivenskey O. Odom – Demetrious Brooks – Marcus McVae – Myron Flowers – Kawaski Trawick – Akeen Brown – Kevin Leroy Beasley – Isaiah Lewis – Ryan Smith – Derrec Jamal Shaw – Sharell Brown – Edward Fuller – Malik Ali Gresham – Pamela Shantay Turner – Ruben Houston – Djuantez Anthony Mitchell – Donald Davis, Jr. –

Daniel Warren – Enosa Strickland – Myles Frazier – Terrance Bridges – Nakia Smith – Curtis Stagger – Crystal Danielle Ragland – Marcus Boles – Miles Hall – Samuel Galberth – Kevin Pudlik – Ryan Twyman – Edtwon Stamps – Rodnell Cotton – Bryan Bernard Wallace – JaQuavion Slaton – Vincense Williams, Jr. – Brent Durbin-Daniel – Jaquan Derrick Dijon Thompson – Brandon Webber – Marquis Weems – Tramon Savage – Mantry Norris – Ty'Rese West – Jamarcus Dejun Moore – Eric Jack Logan – DeWayne Watkins – Jaymil Ellerbe – Bradley Rundle – Elijah Collins III – Marvin Green – Benjamin Ray Smith – Gene Pool – Ben Fields – Isaiah Robinson – Kareem Omar Morgan – Tymar Crawford – Sean Rambert – Darrell Allen – Jamahl Smith – Blige Sean Christopher Cypress – Onaje Dickinson – Dijon D. Watkins – Ashanti Pinkney – Stephen Murray – Roderick Wilson – Leo Brooks – Makeyvion Devonte Cannon – Hashim Jibiri Wilson – Shawan F. Allen – Omari Thompson – Josef Delon Richardson – Jamaal Simpson – Mario Benjamin – Deshon Downing – De'Von Bailey – James Lee Kirkwood – Kaizen Crossen – Detravian Allison – Toussaint Diamon Sims – Jerry Orlando Weaver – Charles Roy Pearson – Rashad Cunningham – Uzzle Jerome – Schaston Theodore Lamarr Hodge – Amari Malone – Michael Tuck – Channara Tom Pheap – Raymond Lewis Williams – Keith Carter – Wallace Wilder – Tyrone Domingo Banks – Terry Tillman – Cortez Shepherd – Vondarrow Dewayne Fisher – Bennie Branch – Quentin Broadus – Bobby Ray Duckworth – Tasjon Tyreek Osbourne – Nicholas Walker – Melvin Watkins – Ronald Davis – Eric Carter – Gregory Edwards – Willie Hudson – Shawn Stevens – Jordan Michael Griffin – Leonard Shand – Jamaal Ramone Taylor – Antonio Williams – Michael John – Maurice Holley – Crederick Joseph – Leo Craig – Sawandi Asad Toussaint – Christopher Whitfield – Victor Jarvis – Nasheem Prioleau – Akinyia Malik Jerome Gray – Lazzeri James Frazier – Allan Feliz – Christopher DeQuan Crosby – Cameron Bennett – Steven Day – Victor Hernandez – Delfon Kinney – Kwesi Ashun – Earnest Easterling –

Dana Sherrod Fletcher – John Feggins – Michael Austin – Maurice Brown – Eddie Ray Maxwell – Treva Smutherman – Shelby Gazaway – Roy McAllister – Treon McCoy – Mark Sheppard – Dante Redmond Jones – Christopher Terrell Willis – Kenneth Simeus – Lance Edward Smith – Ariane Lamont McCree – Nathaniel Pinnock – Micduff Lamarco Robinson – Derrick Everett – Jimmie Phillips – Jerric Harris – Michael Lorenzo Dean – Cameron Lamb – Miguel Russo – Alvern Donnell Walker – Demetrius Williams – Lamar Alexander – Ronnie Jerome Hill – Dominick Matt – Antonio Nichols – Kreed Cornell Bateman – Montay Steven Penning – Francine Graham – David N. Anderson – Cortez Bufford – Taveonte Art Emmanuel – Romello Barnes – Jamee Chrisopher Deonte Johnson – Louis Patrick Veal – Kentrey Marquis Witherspoon – Emanuel Johnson – Steven DeWayne Haizlip – Mohamed Ahemed Al-Hashemi – Romir Talley – Kenneth Collins – Elray Barber – Deangelo Rashad Martin – Antonio Smith – Frederick Perkins – Dedrick Thomas – Malik Williams – Terry Hudson – Jamari Daiwon Tarver – Tyree Davis – Kwamae Jones – Brandon D. Roberts – Michiah Lee – Earl Facey – Claude Fain – Henry Isaac Jones – Ryan O. Simms – Keenan McCain – Renard Antonio Daniels – Albert Lee Hughes – Murbarak Soulemane – Samuel David Mallard – Reginald Leon Boston – Darius J. Tarver – Deandre Lee Seaborough-Patterson – Marquis Golden – Andrew Smyrna – Michael Rivera – D'ovion Semaj Perkins – Joshua James Brown – William Howard Green – Aaron T. Booker – Jaquyn O'Neill Light – Abdirahman Salad – Keith Dutree Collins – Leonard Parker – Ronnell Mouzon – Alvin Cole – Marc Dominic Neal – Darius Tarver – Dominique Antwon Anderson – Jeremy Grayson – Bobby Gibbs – Kevin Adolphe – Joseph Jewell – Kenneth Sashington – Justin Lee Stackhouse – Anthony Taylor – Elijah Jamaal Brewer – Tyler M. Jones – Barry Gedeus – Donnie Sanders – Darwin Foy – William Simpkins – Harold Spencer – Lebarron Ballard – Mycael Johnson – Kamall Koby Edwards – Alvin Lamont Baum – Tyrell Fincher – Etonne Tanzymore – Nathan R.

Hodge – Idris Abdus-Salaam – Dewayne Curtis Lafond – Joshua Dariandre Ruffin – Zyon Romeir Wych – Jonathan Lee Adams – Goldie Bellinger – Jasman Washington – Derick L. Powe – Steven Taylor – Virgill Thrope – Chase Rosa – Elmer L. Mack – Joshua Johnson – Malcolm Xavier Ray Williams – William Debose – Shaun Lee Fuhr – Brent Martin – Said Joquin – Demontre Bruner – Qavon Webb – Jah'Sean Iandie Hodge – Dreasjon Reed – McHale Rose – Adrian Medearis – Finan H. Berhe – Yassin Mohamed – David Tylek Atkinson – Rayshard Scales – Robert Johnson – Randy Roszell – Lewis – Toby Wiggins – Willie Lee Quarles – Maurice S. Gordon – Dion Johnson – Tony McDade – Modesto Reyes – Ruben Smith – Momodou Lamin Sisay – Jarvis Sullivan – Derrick Thompson – David McAtee – Tyquarn Graves – Kamal Flowers – Lewis Ruffin – Michael "Blue" Thomas – Rayshard Brooks – Caine Van Pelt – Terron Jamal Boone – Ky Johnson – Kevan Ruffin – Joseph W. Denton – Hakim Littleton – Vincent Demario Truitt – Darius Washington – Vincent Harris – Southern Jeremy – David Earl Brooks – Darrien Walker

And all those whose names have not been released to protect the privacy of their families or any that were omitted here. Each of their lives mattered!

Every one of these Black people was somebody's child.

Introduction

As I sit here to compose the outline for this book in June of the year 2020, I am concerned yet optimistic about the future of the Black community and our country, the United States of America.

I sit here typing in the midst of a pandemic that has killed tens of thousands of Black Americans and protests of unprecedented scale against police brutality. Businesses going out of business and an unemployment rate the worst it's been since the Great Depression.

At times like this, it can often feel that the world is coming to an end.

But such difficult times are actually unprecedented opportunities to create positive change. Anything that disrupts the normal way of doing things is an opportunity to create a new and better way. Our communities and our nation have finally been shaken free from complacency.

This is an opportunity that many of us have been waiting for a long time. For decades, Black activists have been urging massive change that can create true justice, power, and prosperity in our communities. Many of us have been too wrapped up in ensuring our daily survival to look up and follow them.

Now is the time to look up.

Many of you know me as a serial entrepreneur and a personal development and business mentor to tens of thousands of people across the country over the course of two decades. I champion the cause of progress in the Black community and do my best to advocate for fatherless children and fathers who grew up without a father in their own lives.

My first book, "The Fatherless Father," details my life story as a person who overcame overwhelming obstacles and achieved astounding success with the direction of a strong mother and help from family. More importantly, it provides a road map for parents, children, and communities to raise fatherless Black boys with the confidence, pride, and discipline necessary for success, even when their fathers are not available.

Now is the time to take this work to the next step. We must heal not only our individual Black boys and families, but also our community, culture, and businesses from the traumas inflicted by slavery, colonialism, and systemic racism that continue to this day.

In this book we will discuss specific steps that each of us can take today, and every day, to transform our communities and claim the prosperity that is our birthright. We will cover specific steps that each of us can act upon on a daily or weekly basis that will allow us to:

1. Create a new world where Black people are no longer killed by police.

2. Build up Black men and boys with the senses of confidence, pride, and responsibility that create potential for boundless success.

3. Create wealth and prosperity for our children to inherit and give them every advantage in life.

4. Create a culture of success that opens new doors for our children.

5. Become leaders in our own communities who are capable of creating real, lasting change, both legal and financial.

6. Become politically involved in a way that allows us to make real, meaningful changes to the laws that govern our cities, our states, and our nation.

7. Collaborate and cooperate in ways that uplift the *national and*

global Black communities – not just individuals and isolated families.

8. Accomplish real reparations in the form of lasting financial and material compensation for the extreme costs of slavery, colonialism, Jim Crow, and continued racism and discrimination to our families.

9. Get it done.

To make these solutions a reality, it is necessary to discuss the roots of the challenges we face today.

We'll discuss the effects of slavery and discrimination which can make it feel impossible to imagine a better world, or to imagine that our actions can really create such a world. We'll discuss exactly how high the cost of racism is to our children and our communities, and exactly how urgent it is that we take real action to fight with everything we have within us to create a better world.

We'll discuss the government's history of failing us – and how we can take matters into our own hands by taking the necessary steps to build a culture that fully develops the limitless potential of our children, to build wealth that will support them in their work, and even in some cases to *become* the government by prying open the doors of the electoral system.

I am honored that you have chosen to come along with me on this journey. This book is both a deeply heartfelt and personal plea from me – a Black man who grew up as a Black boy surrounded by the high cost of racism – and a community blueprint informed by the work of some of the greatest researchers and teachers of our time on these subjects.

I hope that I will someday meet or speak to many of you at one of my live seminar events, mentorship meetups, book signings, business meetings, or maybe even see you at the ballot box.

Regardless, we can do this. We will overcome and win. Together.

Chapter 1

Ending Police Brutality

"I contend that the cry of 'black power' is, at bottom, a reaction to the reluctance of white power to make the kind of changes necessary to make justice a reality for the Negro. I think that we've got to see that a riot is the language of the unheard. And, what is it that America has failed to hear?"

–Martin Luther King, Jr.

Almost any American Black person will tell you that police brutality in this country is out of control. Many of us – perhaps most – have personally known someone who was shot, beaten, held at gunpoint by law enforcement officers, incarcerated, or died under suspicious circumstances. Many of us fear to call the police for help, anxious that someone might end up shot, killed, or unjustly arrested due to police intervention.

It is difficult for those who aren't Black in America to understand just how real this fear is. While some insist that these killings are "justified," we can often feel unsafe simply walking outside in our own skin.

The good news is, in this present moment we face unprecedented capacity for change. The protests of the last few months have been called the most widespread protest movement in American history. A majority of Americans of all races now support the cause of Black Lives Matter, and perhaps for the first time in history, serious consideration is being given by lawmakers to reforms that could really improve our situation.

In this chapter we'll discuss some specific pieces of legislation which are being promoted by Black activists to end police brutality, and how you can help ensure that these laws are passed by your city and state lawmakers. We'll also take a moment to discuss the roots of this problem: roots which reach back into an American history we may never have been taught in schools.

The Roots of Police Brutality

Many activists have stated, rightly so, that police brutality is not just a matter of local police department corruption. Though many problems have been identified with how police are trained today, and with the laws they are taught to enforce, the roots of these problems reach much further back than the origins of your local police academy.

We all know about slavery. What we might not realize is the extent to which the American economy as we know it today has always been based on the unpaid and forced labor of Black people.

The concept of "whiteness," for example, is only a few hundred years old. Prior to the colonization of the New World, French, German, and English people would have looked at you like you were crazy if you suggested that they were all of the same race. Like all traditional peoples, traditional Europeans took pride in their familial, cultural, and national ancestry: not in the color of their skin.

However, when Europe began to colonize Africa, Asia, and the Americas the European powers began to run into a problem. They didn't want to go to war with their neighbors, who shared land borders with them and were just as well-armed as themselves. Why bother, when there was so much wealth for the taking on other continents, held by people who lived too far away to invade their homelands?

A method had to be developed for deciding who had legal rights – that is, who might carry a high cost if they were attacked or exploited – and who did not have legal rights under the European system.

Europeans – especially the northern and western European powers who possessed the world's largest navies, armies, and guns at the time – were all pale-skinned. And so, the idea of "whiteness" as an attribute which granted a person legal rights and privileges anywhere in the world was invented.

Those who were *not* white, on the other hand, were fair game for enslavement, exploitation, rape, and murder if the white colonists deemed it convenient or desirable. People of color often had absolutely no legal standing in colonial European governments and could be disposed of and threatened in any matter seen fitting by European governors.

There is no better example of this attitude than the clause in the United States Constitution which states that Black people count as three-fifths of a person for population counting purposes.

Why did we even get that three-fifths of legal standing? Purely because the governors of slave-holding states wanted more power to influence laws in the American Congress. By demanding the "three-fifths compromise," they were able to count Black people among the reasons they deserved more legislative power – all while simultaneously treating us as property, and giving that legislative power to the white land-owning men who *could* vote to implement their own desires in our names.

They did this, of course, because their entire economy was based on our unpaid and forced labor. The wealth of the American South came from the strength of Black arms, legs, and minds, even as white slave owners claimed ownership of and credit for everything our ancestors produced and murdered any enslaved Black people who thought about claiming credit for themselves.

But even in the three-fifths compromise, there was hope. The white lawmakers and land owners of slave-owning states were trying everything to consolidate their power at the national level for a very good reason: already there were some states that did not tolerate slavery within their borders, and which tried at every turn to outlaw it at the national level. The battle between slave owners and abolitionists would, of course, come to a head in the Civil War.

The American Civil War *was* about slavery. Don't let anyone tell you otherwise. While some claim that it was about "state's rights" or "local autonomy," the real issue was the refusal of slave owners to recognize the humanity of Black people.

Doing so threatened to take their sources of wealth – our ancestors – right out from under them. So, they wouldn't do it. They even took up arms against their own national government to fight for the right to keep profiting off of our ancestors' labor, while keeping our ancestors in states of fear that made it difficult to fight back.

After the Civil War, slavery was made illegal throughout the U.S....allegedly.

President Abraham Lincoln formally issued the Emancipation Proclamation on January 1, 1863, calling on the Union army to liberate all slaves. But it wasn't until June 19, 1865 when Union army general Gordon Granger made it to Galveston, Texas and announced federal orders proclaiming that all slaves were free.

Today June 19th is a day celebrated as marking the end of slavery for Blacks all across the nation, known as Juneteenth. But other ways for wealthy white landowners to effectively own Black people and prevent us from gaining any control over the fruits of our own labors soon sprung up.

The practice of sharecropping made Black families technically free – as long as they paid outrageous, often impossible taxes and fees to white landowners. When sharecroppers inevitably failed to pay the arbitrary and unregulated costs, they were considered to be "in debt" – and were seen in the eyes of the law as debtors who had failed to pay their bills of their own free will, and who were therefore fair game for coercion, incarceration, and more.

After sharecropping was abolished due to popular demand, the era of Jim Crow was ushered in.

Under Jim Crow laws – a system of both actual, on-the-books laws and unspoken, unwritten, social agreements between white people – Black people could be punished by any means, including death, for such "crimes" as being too financially successful, attempting to gain access to the social spaces of successful whites, and generally being too bold or successful in reaching for equality, success, or power of any kind.

This was the era of lynchings: when Black people, usually men, could be executed by mobs, law enforcement, or individuals with few to no legal consequences. These lynchings often took place outside of the law. There were no longer laws on the books which permitted these killings of Black people, yet no legal action was taken against the killers.

The era of Jim Crow ended, in theory, during the Civil Rights era of the mid-20th century. During this time, tougher laws such as the Civil Rights Act were passed which were designed to mandate legal punishment for anyone who discriminated against Black people or punished them for success.

This Act was passed into law through the tireless work of millions of Black activists, protesters, and voters. Using every legal advantage provided to them, millions of Black people worked together to create boycotts, sit-ins, marches, and other acts that demonstrated the power of the Black community to create wealth.

These demonstrations reminded America just how essential Black labor was to its economy and prompted many lawmakers to change their tunes to meet the demands of Black workers and voters around the country.

The Civil Rights Act was groundbreaking legislation, and the legal basis of most subsequent laws and court decisions in favor of Black people fighting violence and discrimination for the past half-century.

It was also an example of the fact that, when Black people fight for equality in an organized, disciplined, and informed manner, things really do get better. Imagine telling a slave living during the Civil War in 1864 that, as of 1964, it would be illegal to discriminate against him in any way because he was Black.

But as we've seen, the letter of the law is never the full story. And despite the passage of the Civil Rights Act, the fight was far from over. As it still is to this day.

Just as with sharecropping, wealthy and powerful white politicians and business owners soon found ways to avail themselves of the profits of forced Black labor. These loopholes took a few forms which are important for Black people of today to know about.

Redlining and Housing Discrimination

Even when it was technically illegal to discriminate on a basis of race, landlords, realtors, and other property brokers often systematically found ways to deny property in wealthy neighborhoods to Black families.

These property brokers might state – truthfully or not – that they had received better offers or turned down Black buyers for other reasons. But the truth was, institutional racism was at work while hiding its true appearance. Many property sellers assumed that Black buyers would be more likely to damage property, less likely to pay their bills, or that wealthy families that could pay high prices for housing would not want to live next to Black families.

The result was that, while racist motives in these sales were often hidden and therefore immune from prosecution under the law, to this day the maps of "most dangerous" and "poorest" neighborhoods often overlap almost precisely with maps of "black majority" neighborhoods.

Dangers found in neighborhoods where Black families have been allowed to live can include toxins in the air, water, and soil which increase the risk of health problems; more racist and corrupt police departments; and...

Underfunded Schools

Many Americans don't know that the majority of public school funding in the U.S. comes from property taxes. Do you see the obvious problem with this? In a country where the majority of Black people live in the most low-income and least-desired neighborhoods, most Black people *also* live in neighborhoods with the lowest property tax revenues in the country.

This means that schools in Black neighborhoods are overwhelmingly drastically underfunded. And despite frequent attempts to bring this issue to national attention, these issues have continued.

A huge percentage of Black public schools are considered "effectively segregated" – though there are no laws against racial diversity and the schools may have some white students, the majority of students – often 90%+ – belong to racial minorities.

These "majority minority" schools are well-known to have dismal funding, overwhelmed teachers, infeasibly large class sizes, and often dangerously under-maintained physical infrastructure such as unacceptably high levels of neurotoxic lead in drinking water and paint, dangerous mold which can exacerbate health conditions, and broken chairs, desks, and banisters that place children at greater risk for injury and reduce their ability to concentrate on learning.

These dangerously underfunded public schools in "majority minority" neighborhoods are the first step in what scholars call the "school to prison pipeline." Considered by many to be a new form of slavery or sharecropping, the school to prison pipeline is a system where Black children are systematically given inferior educations and inferior job opportunities, all while being policed by racist and corrupt departments enforcing racist and irrational laws.

Has this "school to prison pipeline" affected someone you know? Maybe several someones who have ended up incarcerated despite being intelligent and good people? If you are Black in America, the answer is almost certainly "yes."

And there's a good chance that those people were affected by the next step in the school-to-prison pipeline, namely...

The War on Drugs

Drugs are bad. It's true. Heroin, crack cocaine, and methamphetamine are among the leading causes of destroyed lives in the Black community. Once these highly addictive substances have been tasted, it can be nearly impossible for people to stop buying and using them without medical and community support that is often sorely lacking in Black neighborhoods.

And yet, any neuroscientist or public health expert will tell you that the American government's "War on Drugs" is not actually crafted to create better public health outcomes or to eliminate drug use. In fact, its laws don't make any scientific sense.

A number of 20th century politicians and political advisors have all-but admitted that the anti-drug legislation of the 20th century was crafted, not to improve public health, but to break up the Black Power and hippie movements. Many drugs which were outlawed, such as marijuana, showed little to no potential for harm or addictiveness, and even showed positive effects when used with discernment to treat many medical and mental health conditions.

But if the government could arrest people who used these drugs – which were popular among both the Black Power and hippie movements – it could destroy the political power of those movements and demonize them in the eyes of the public.

Legal moves like incarcerating people over marijuana use or punishing possession of crack cocaine orders of magnitude more harshly than powdered cocaine had no basis in medical science. But they did have the effect of allowing law enforcement to incarcerate millions of Black people, all while claiming that these people were criminals who were much more dangerous than the white Wall Street bankers and rock stars who openly glorified powdered cocaine.

In recent decades, we have finally begun to see some of these laws being rolled back. Through the tireless work of Black activists, organizers, and voters, unequal sentencing laws have been challenged and marijuana has been re-legalized in some states. Some states have even seriously discussed plans to release people incarcerated under drug laws that are now recognized as unfair and unscientific.

People who are mostly Black, of course.

Imagine what we could accomplish if every single Black person in this country were actively involved in the city council and state legislature meetings where these legal moves are discussed. Imagine what would happen if we paid as much attention to these laws, how they are made, and how they are changed, as we do to our personal and family business.

We'll discuss more of how to make this vision a reality in later chapters.

Before we get to solutions, there are a few more important causes of Black oppression and police brutality that are important to understand. These include...

Racist Police Education and Hiring Policies

Many people have asked why it is that so many police officers seem to behave in racist ways. Is it that policing attracts racist and violent people? Maybe. But many former police officers have also raised alarms in recent months about the training they received as police recruits.

Former police officers have reported being instilled with the idea that the world – the communities they were policing – were out to get them. Many, such as the anonymous author of the Medium article "Confessions of a Former Bastard Cop," report being shown hundreds of videos of police being shot by civilians – the people they're supposed to serve and protect – and being told that this would happen to them if they ever let their guard down.

While the claims of anonymous author "Officer A. Cab" are shocking, they are not new. Dave Grossman, former U.S. Air Force Lieutenant Colonel who now trains police officers, openly describes himself as a "Professor of Killology." He boasts that his trainings "make it possible [for his police officer students] to kill without conscious thought."

In his trainings, Grossman emphasizes that police officers must loosen their inhibitions around killing and be prepared to take a life at any moment if they are to successfully survive and defend innocent people in the line of duty.

It's perhaps easy to understand, then, why many police officers who receive such training could become trigger-happy when faced with unarmed Black people.

Many officers may be in the position of the officer who shot Black therapist Charles Kinsey while Kinsey was trying to de-escalate a confrontation between police and his autistic Black patient who the officers saw as a threat. When Kinsey (who fortunately survived) asked the officer who shot him: "Why did you shoot me," the officer looked bewildered.

His response? "I don't know."

This officer, like so many others, had been conditioned to see the people he was supposed to protect – especially black people, as threats to his own life. Despite the fact that Kinsey and his patient were both clearly unarmed, he saw these two Black men as a threat.

To make matters worse, many officers have also reported being threatened by their own colleagues and supervisors for reporting or refusing to engage in racist behavior.

The threat that "you might not get backup when you need it" – that other cops would not act to protect cops who refused to corroborate lies about Black suspects or who spoke up against racist violence in the department – is commonly reported among former police officers in both the United States and Canada.

Millions of Black activists and organizers are pushing legislation to improve these situations, and for the first time, many city councils and voter populations seem to be taking these laws seriously. We'll discuss some of these laws, and how you can put pressure on your city council to pass them, later.

For those Black people who survive their encounters with the police over drugs or other causes, the last stop in the school-to-prison pipeline is...

Private and For-Profit Prisons

Did you know that prisons are allowed to force incarcerated people to work for just a few cents per hour in compensation? Did you also know that many of these prisons are privately owned, and are allowed to profit off of the work of these inmates?

Does this system sound familiar at all?

News of modern-day slavery – which is *supposed* to be legally colorblind, but is in practice composed of a majority of Black people due to the racist practices described above – has hit the news headlines in recent years. News stories in which judges accepted bribes to sentence Black youth to long terms in for-profit prisons – effectively selling these youth into slavery – have gained national attention.

The fact that the United States has more prisoners than China – a country with over three times our population and an infamously authoritarian government – has also become more widely known.

While many members of the public are outraged that American people are being used as forced labor for wealthy prison owners, many don't know how to help change this situation.

We'll explore how *you* can help to abolish for-profit prisons, racist policing practices, and racist drug laws in the sections of this book to come.

How To Help

All of these are laws which can make the situation feel hopeless when we as individuals try to fight against violence and injustices we witness in our own lives.

And yet, *all of these are laws which can be changed.* Like the Civil Rights activists before us, we can force legislatures to change the laws that oppress us.

But we can do this *only* if we work together, as one.

Only when every single Black person in America becomes involved in this strategy, embraces their great power and great responsibility, and becomes educated about how to use their limitless potential to make real change, will we see the change we need to make a better future for our children.

Calling and writing our politicians and demanding that they solve school funding issues, racist drug legislation, police brutality, and for-profit prisons is easy to do. In fact, because few people participate in city councils and state legislatures, it can be surprisingly easy for educated citizens to take control of these legislative bodies and obtain major influence in the creation and enforcement of city and state laws.

Here are some laws which have already been developed by activists and policy experts who have been working for decades to solve these problems.

I encourage each and every one of you to take a pause at the end of this chapter, and research which of these pieces of legislation your city and state already have, which they are considering implementing, and which are not even on their radar.

When we unify to vote, protest, engage in civil disobedience to make our demands heard, and strengthen our financial positions to make governments and businesses listen, we can produce rapid change. This is proven by the dozens of laws to improve racist policing practices which have already been passed by city councils around the country in the past few months.

Let's keep pushing. Let's make ourselves impossible to ignore.

Defund the Police

You may have heard that the slogan "Defund the Police" has gained unprecedented popularity in recent months. At first, this slogan might sound scary. If there is no police department, who will maintain law and order? But in fact, that's not what this legislation seeks to accomplish.

The activists and policy experts behind "Defund the Police" have pointed out that police department funding often drastically outpaces funding for social services, mental health crisis support, housing for the homeless, and other services that are arguably more appropriate for responding to many police calls. In fact, the police department budgets of many American cities are similar to the military budgets of entire *countries* around the world.

Even many police officers have stated that they do not always feel that comfortable responding as armed, combat-trained enforcers to calls about mental health crises, drug use crises, domestic violence, welfare checks, and more. In police academies, training about conflict de-escalation, mental health, homelessness, and more are often treated as afterthoughts to training about combat, use of force, and self-defense. This is a recipe for disaster.

For that reason, "Defund the Police" legislation focuses on cutting police department funding and moving that funding to the creation of emergency on-call teams that provide services like:

1. Mental health crisis experts trained in de-escalating suicidal and threatening behavior.

2. Social workers trained in helping people get access to resources such as housing, food stamps, and healthcare, lack of which may underlie many public safety situations.

3. Crisis de-escalation experts who are primarily trained in "talking down" people showing threatening or violent behavior without the need for weapons.

4. Homelessness assistance and housing programs, which have been proven to improve employment rates and public health outcomes, and save cities large amounts of money that would otherwise be spent on law enforcement and emergency medicine services for homelessness-related situations.

In June of 2020, the city council of Minneapolis made history by being one of the first cities in the United States to adopt "Defund the Police" legislation and take serious action toward addressing mental health, poverty, and homelessness in a scientific and humanitarian way, rather than treating all of these as primarily criminal problems.

Consider calling or writing to your city councilperson, or even showing up in person to your local city council meetings, to support similar legislation in your hometown.

8 To Abolition

"8 to Abolition" is a package of laws designed to abolish the slavery-like institutions that still exist in our country today. The eight steps included in this legislative plan are designed to create more community investment, autonomy, and empowerment in black communities while eliminating racist policing, racist law enforcement, and racist laws themselves.

The 8 steps advocated by these abolitionists include:

1. Defund the Police, as described above, is the first step.

2. Demilitarize Communities. Many Americans don't realize that in the wake of the Iraq and Afghanistan wars, many municipal police forces purchased full-on military warfare equipment for use against their own citizens.

   Even residents of relatively small towns may find themselves faced with military assault vehicles, flashbang grenades (originally an urban warfare tactic), and more if they are deemed disorderly or threatening to the local law enforcement. This doesn't help the situation.

   Demilitarization involves removing this equipment from our cities, cutting funds used to purchase it, and cultivating an attitude of "Protect and Serve" – the official police slogan – rather than the attitude that the people of the community are the enemy of the police.

3. Remove Police from Schools. While some communities once pushed for better security for their students in the wake of school shootings and other threats, many troubling videos have since surfaced of students being physically abused and brutalized by police officers in schools.

   Reports of elementary school children being arrested for disorderly conduct, disabled children being seriously injured by school police, and school officer's guns being inappropriately fired during school hours have prompted calls to take police out of schools, where they often seem to do more harm than good.

4. Free People from Jails and Prisons. Proponents of "8 to Abolish" support freeing people from disproportionate prison sentences and pursuing models of justice based on rehabilitation and community restoration, rather than brutal punishment.

   Many analysts have noted that our modern prison system often makes offenders *worse* by housing minor and nonviolent offenders in close and poorly monitored quarters with experienced, hardened, violent criminals.

   Today's prisons also fail miserably at equipping prisoners to succeed in legal professions after incarceration. In fact, almost half of U.S. people who have been imprisoned are imprisoned again within one year of release, often on more serious charges than the ones that they were initially imprisoned for.

5. Repeal Laws that Criminalize Survival. One under-appreciated factor in incarceration and harm to our communities is the "criminalization of homelessness." Many cities and states have laws under which people can be imprisoned simply for sleeping on public or private property or collecting bottles and cans for recycling money.

   This approach benefits the for-profit prison system, but not community members who may someday find themselves imprisoned for lack of ability to afford housing. The idea that those who can't pay rent can be forced into work for for-profit prisons certainly does begin to seem like a system designed to force Black people to work for billionaires while being drastically undercompensated for their labor.

6. Invest in Community Self-Governance. By taking measures to increase the legal power and civic participation of local communities, we can provide alternatives to racist policing by outside forces.

   Whether it's fighting plans to tear down community spaces for profit or fighting local police departments that incarcerate up to 33% of all Black men at some point in their lives, taking action to educate ourselves about what community self-governance looks like and to make it a reality is an investment in all our children's futures.

7. Providing safe housing for everyone. As mentioned above, trials studies have shown that free housing programs for the homeless actually *profit* local communities by improving public health and safety, improving local employment rates, *and* saving public funds for emergency medical care and law enforcement.

   That makes providing safe housing for everyone not just the right thing to do – but the profitable thing for our communities, as well.

8. Invest in Care, Not Cops. This takes the tenants of "Defund the Police" to the next level. By investing in safe housing, mental and medical healthcare, crisis de-escalation, and restorative justice, we can make our communities safer, healthier, and wealthier, all while drastically reducing police violence and incarceration.

I recommend that you take a look at whether your local city has an activism movement devoted to making "8 to Abolition" a reality in your community today.

We could be standing at the cusp of the next Civil Rights movement – but only if *we* make it so.

Civilian Police Accountability Councils

Another reform promoted by many opponents of police brutality is the creation of "Civilian Police Accountability Councils" or CPACs – councils made of civilian community members which review and have a voice in police brutality cases.

Many communities have felt left out in the cold when local police departments tell them that cases of police brutality or suspicious deaths have been "reviewed" – by a department internal to the police department, with a vested interest in protecting the department's budgets and officers, in hearings conducted behind closed doors.

As a result, a growing number of city councils have been considering creating CPACs to ease public concerns about policing practices and reduce police violence in communities.

While police unions and departments often fight fiercely against the creation of CPACs, claiming that these councils might impair officers' ability to protect themselves and others, many activists have asked why police departments seem to feel that the ability to do violence against the citizens they are supposed to protect and serve is necessary to do their jobs.

I encourage you to look to see if your city has a Civilian Police Accountability Council – and if not, who in your local area is pushing for one to be created, and how you can help them – today.

The End Goal

Legislation is always a complex matter. Lawmakers and lobbyists will argue endlessly over the letter of the law, and precisely what the law should and should not permit. These discussions can feel boring or overwhelming for those of us who may be pouring everything we have just into building wealth and safety for ourselves and our immediate families.

But when we work together – when we allocate that extra time, energy, and inconvenience into learning how to help our community – we create communities where *all* of us struggle less and receive more safety, more support, and more power.

Isn't that what all of us want for our children? Safety, support, and power?

We accomplish much more when we work together as one than we ever could as individuals. None of us can hope to *individually* change the law, the prison system, or the school system. But all of us *together* have enough power to create transformative changes in our neighborhoods, our cities, and our country.

How do we motivate ourselves to keep putting forth this work on a daily, weekly, and monthly basis?

We keep the end goal insight.

No more Black boys or girls shot or killed by the cops.

No more communities where up to one third of Black men are incarcerated.

No more communities where we are afraid to have our children leave the house because they might be targeted for police violence.

Our end goal is safety, prosperity, and autonomy for our children and our communities.

Isn't that a goal worth fighting for?

Chapter 2

The Fatherless Epidemic, Its Impact, and Its Origins

"When I grew up, my uncles and grandfather were always supportive of me. They gave me the attention I needed from a man. [...] Yes, my mother was my primary caregiver, but she knew (as I slowly began to realize during my formative years) that there was advice she wouldn't be able to give me but knew those men could."

–Reco M. McCambry, "The Fatherless Father"

My first book, "The Fatherless Father," described the impact of fatherlessness on my life and the lives of other Black boys. Growing up without a father myself, I longed for a father like the one I saw on the Cosby Show.

Why didn't I get to have a family like that? I wondered. Why couldn't my father behave in that way? Was there something wrong with me? Was there something wrong with my father?

My mother had the wisdom to ensure that I was surrounded by other kind, strong, and wise Black men to serve as role models for me. My grandfather and uncles all taught me important lessons about being a man.

From my PawPaw I learned wisdom, commitment, and discipline. From my uncle Kevin I learned confidence, pride, and charm. From my uncle Orsola I learned to appreciate nature, cultivate my connection to it, and live off the land. From my uncle June I learned about women, sexuality, and learned to navigate the often questionable landscape of modern media.

The impact of these men in my life was far more important than the specific lessons they taught me. They also showed me *examples.*

They did not merely talk the talk: they also walked the walk, *showing* me that it really was possible for Black men to live out all these virtues, practice all of these skills, and become any sort of man imaginable. Without them in my life, I might have doubted my abilities as a Black boy, or the likelihood that I could create a future of achievement, commitment, and success.

If they could do it, it was possible for me too.

Recent research has underscored this personal story, showing that *all* children do better when they have strong, caring, positive adults of their own race and gender in their lives growing up. In fact, it's been found that children of *all* races and genders do better when they have examples of caring, supportive, strong Black men in their families and schools.

Our society is just beginning to understand the power of role models. For many years we thought it was enough to *tell* our children they could be anything. But it turns out, we have to *show* them. Children form subconscious conclusions about the world based on what they see. What they observe happening in the world is at least as influential as the words of the adults around them.

Some recent studies have shown that even brief interventions can drastically change the behaviors and career paths of Black children – as long as those interventions are led by Black role models, including men.

Experiments in sending Black children to Black-led schools, summer camps, and other programs have shown that these interventions can transform a child's academic career and future work life by improving their confidence and motivation to study math, science, and other subjects children might once have considered unrealistic. Simply the effect of seeing people like yourself modeling success can be astounding.

It seems that the key to many of our community's problems lie in a lack of fathers. But how did this situation happen? Are Black people, as some suggest, just less interested in being fathers or positive role models?

The answer to that is a resounding "NO!" Just like with incarceration and forced labor, the history of fatherlessness in the Black community stretches back hundreds of years, and is propagated by legal and cultural policies from outside the Black community that continue to actively break up families and take our fathers away.

So how can we fight this epidemic, if its roots lie outside of our own communities?

The same way we fight for everything else. We resist these policies to the greatest extent we are able in our personal lives – and we work together to change the laws and the culture of our entire nation.

The Origin of Family Separation

Many of you may have heard that Black fatherlessness, like so many other problems plaguing our communities, began during the slave trade. White slave owners who knew that they needed to keep their slaves frightened, disorganized, and powerless would regularly break up families to prevent enslaved Black people from organizing the sorts of family units that could nurture the seeds of rebellion against their oppressors.

By separating fathers from their wives and children and children from their mothers, slave owners kept enslaved Black people demoralized, scared, and traumatized. It was common for married Black couples to be specifically broken up, and for children to be sold to slave owners in other cities and states, far away from their mothers, as soon as they were old enough to work.

Indeed, some of you may have heard that the "jumping the broom" wedding tradition arose because enslaved Black people were often not allowed to have church weddings or to marry legally. As property, they had no legal rights associated with marriage, and white religious institutions avoided recognizing any humanity in Black enslaved people at all.

The patterns created by slavery have had devastating effects on the Black community down the generations. With many Black enslaved boys growing up with no father figures, many then lacked parenting skills themselves when legal changes made it theoretically impossible for them to stay with their families. Some Black enslaved men even internalized the examples of their white owners who believed that power was best expressed through violence, not love.

As you might have guessed, Black fatherhood didn't magically become easy when slavery ended. Sharecroppers faced many of the same dangers and traumas as enslaved people. They often lacked power to protect their families from white violence, and the idea that Black men were not able to provide for their families was actively spread by landlords who wanted society to view Black men as incapable of productive labor, and therefore deserving of debt and forced labor.

This, of course, was a vicious lie. In reality, the very reason white landlords spread this myth of the deadbeat sharecropper was *because the sharecropper's labor was so productive.* If white people wanted to keep sitting back and reaping the fruits of Black labor, they had to make everyone – especially Black people – believe that Black men were not capable of providing for or raising strong families.

As sharecropping was outlawed and the Civil Rights Act was passed, white billionaires and politicians found a new, sneaky way to continue separating Black families. Surprisingly, this came in the form of the welfare system.

Public welfare benefits are a staple of any civilized society. Societies which don't provide medical care, food, housing, and other basic human rights to their people end up with epidemics of preventable illness, starvation, and people dying in the streets. So when legislation was proposed to provide new benefits to Americans who were struggling to pay their bills, this was seen as a step in the right direction.

However, racist powers found ways to sneak into even these pieces of legislation, by putting *conditions* on the receipt of these benefits.

In many cases, benefits such as Medicaid, food stamps, and housing assistance depended on one thing: fatherlessness. The laws were often written so that families would lose access to these essential benefits if they had a father living in the home, or if the family's income was too high.

It was easy for politicians to argue that this was a simple matter of cost-savings. Surely a two-parent household didn't need help affording these basic essentials – unless the parents were lazy deadbeats. Right? So it was just good fiscal sense to offer these benefits only to single-parent homes.

This logic, of course, was just one more cover story for racism. It ignored the systemic challenges from racist housing practices, racist school funding, racist policing, and racist incarceration. It ignored the centuries of oppression that had left Black people unable to own land, vote, accumulate wealth, attend good schools, or be hired into high-paying jobs for most of American history.

The implication that poverty was a result of laziness was one of the most pernicious lies of the 20th century. It completely ignored most of American history – and the fact that a huge amount of white wealth had in fact been created by Black hands.

The 20th century was rife with tragic stories, many of which you probably know personally.

The man who wanted to marry the mother of his children, but couldn't because she would have lost Medicaid coverage for herself and their children if he did. The man who then couldn't get custody of his children when their mother died, forcing them into foster care, because he was not legally their father.

The family that had to hide their father's existence when the authorities performed housing inspections, because if they were found to have a father living with them they would have lost their housing assistance. The way that made their father feel – like his family was safer if he wasn't around or involved in their lives.

Some particularly savvy racist politicians have even tried to use these stories to argue that *all* welfare programs are bad, and that housing assistance, Medicaid, and food stamps should be done away with entirely. This of course is nonsensical – creating more homeless, sick, and hungry children is to no one's benefit.

In the chapters to come, we'll learn how to raise our level of wealth to a point where these programs will no longer be necessary for most Black families – but safety nets to allow our disabled and unfortunate brothers and sisters to access food, healthcare, and education will always be necessary.

Lies like these are the reason why we as Black people *must* be highly involved in political participation.

We must show up to city council meetings and state legislature meetings. We must vote in municipal, state, and federal elections. We might fight voter suppression laws (which modern analysts say are "surgically targeted" at Black communities) to ensure our voices are heard. We must educate ourselves about the laws that are being passed, and make ourselves impossible to ignore while advocating the laws that will improve our children's futures.

Whether perpetrated through slavery, sharecropping, or welfare requirements, fatherlessness has scarred our communities in incredible ways. Here are just a few acute problems arising from fatherlessness which we as Black people must watch out for and actively work against in our families and communities.

Black Boys Who Don't Know Their Worth

When Black boys are raised without fathers in their lives, it's easy for their self-concepts to be limited. If they don't have any examples of caring, strong, successful Black men in their daily lives, it's easy for children to conclude that such men simply can't exist.

I always remember the story of one little Black boy who met President Barack Obama. Staring in amazement, confusion, and shock, the little boy asked Obama to bend over so that he could feel his hair. The President obliged, and the little boy ran his fingers over Barack Obama's scalp.

"His hair really is just like mine!" the little boy exclaimed in awe. He was having difficulty believing that the President of the United States could really look like him and have hair like his, after a lifetime of seeing only white men portrayed as Presidents.

I grew up knowing that Black men could and did have caring, strong, committed marriages that lasted a lifetime. My grandfather was a part of my life, and he did all that. I grew up knowing that Black men could be confident, suave, and well-loved. My uncle Kevin spent lots of time with me, and he was all of those things. I grew up knowing that Black men could live off the land, be outdoorsmen, and appreciate nature. My uncle Orsola did all of those things, and he took me fishing all the time.

Yet still, I suffered from anger, bitterness, and doubt. Because I did not have a father in my life, I wondered if I was worthy of a father's love. I wondered if my father – and by extension, me – was incapable of certain types of caring, commitment, and responsibility. I wondered if I would grow up to be like him – absent from my children's lives – or if committing to raise a family was too hard.

Now imagine if I had grown up *without* my uncles or PawPaw in my life. If my *only* models of caring, strength, and responsibility all wrapped into one were my mother and the fathers I saw on TV. What might I have concluded about my potential as a Black boy? What behaviors might I have learned were normal, expected, and necessary for boys who looked like me?

Black boys who lack positive Black men in their lives grow up drastically underestimating their own worth. If they don't see Black men behaving in caring and supportive ways, handling money responsibly, and obtaining success, they might assume that it's not possible or reasonable for them to do so as adults.

One cannot fault a child for learning from the world around him. Which is why it's up to us, as Black adults, to make sure that the world our children see around them is the best possible world.

Black Girls Who Don't Know Their Worth

As we all know, it's not just Black boys who are affected by fatherlessness. Black girls suffer too when they don't have strong male role models, protectors, and teachers.

"Daddy issues" are a cultural cliche at this point. Yet, it is also true and important that young women may form their opinions of what behavior they should accept from men based on the behavior of their fathers.

Black girls who grow up without fathers may assume that they are unworthy of a man's love. They may feel that it's their job to work hard and offer up all manner of favors to please men. The idea that men must also please *them* and win *their* approval might never occur to them. Because they did not grow up with the constant love and support of Black men, they may assume that expecting constant love and support from a male partner is unrealistic.

If we want our Black girls to know their worth, we must ensure that they learn this from Black men as well as Black women. When our girls have father figures to teach them that they deserve love and respect from men and that they can and *should* hold the men in their lives to high standards of behavior, they *believe* these things. They feel it in their bones because they have *seen* that this is possible, rather than just being told about it.

Black boys and girls alike learn what is responsible for them based on the world we show them. They develop their beliefs about themselves and their expectations of themselves and others based on the examples they see around them.

So let's set the best possible examples for our Black girls and boys. Let's not just *tell* them that they can be anything they want to be – like President Barack Obama, let's *show* them.

Lack of Generational Wealth

So far, we have shared a lot of pretty words about what is possible. But many of you may be feeling a sort of itch in the back of your minds. "It's all well and good that this is *possible*, Reco," you might be saying. "But is it *realistic?* Can I do everything that's necessary to build this brighter future, *and* still pay the bills?"

Lack of generational wealth is arguably the single most important component of racism and the oppression of Black people. Everyone knows that poverty plagues the Black community and is a prime factor in its problems, including fatherlessness. However, many people don't fully connect *why* this is the case. The destructive myth that "poverty happens because of laziness or lack of ability" is so widespread that even many of us may believe it on a subconscious level.

In fact, as we've seen, we often lack generational wealth because it has been *stolen* from us. Enslaved Black people contributed huge amounts of wealth to this nation – but that wealth was taken, controlled, and passed down through the generations by white landowners. The labor of sharecroppers was so profitable and productive that white landowners found legal loopholes that allowed them to control that wealth.

The labor of Black minimum wage workers and incarcerated people continues to be hugely profitable to this day. Why else would billionaires and politicians fight so hard to maintain conditions where we are forced to work for them, while being paid only pennies on the dollar for what we produce?

When we put it this way, it can sound hopeless. So much wealth has been taken from Black communities by white billionaires and governments – how can we ever catch up?

And yet, this story also gives us hope. Our labor is *so* profitable that the powers that be will do almost anything to control us.

What would happen if we invested in educating ourselves about how to create wealth *while working for ourselves?* What would happen if we learned the proper legal channels and business practices to keep all of that value *for ourselves?* What would happen if we learned the same secrets of investing, land ownership, and other tricks that white nobles and billionaires have been teaching their children for generations?

Well, I am a pretty good example of what happens when a Black man takes those steps. By working for myself and cultivating personal development, business skills, and legal knowhow, I became a multi-million dollar producing businessman while still in my twenties.

The children of financially successful individuals can receive every benefit of that wealth, including the best education – both the academic education needed for the highest-paying careers in the United States, and the practical and legal application that wealthy people pass on to their children. Their children will inherit land, houses, college funds, and more. So will their grandchildren and great-grandchildren.

I am blessed for my family to experience and look forward to these benefits. I have been one of the lucky few who was exposed to the correct inspiration, education, and opportunities at the right time, enabling me to make this leap. I firmly believe that any other member of the Black community is capable of doing the same – if only they can surround themselves with the knowledge and influences which are so often denied to Black Americans by certain public schools and popular culture. Despite these obstacles, as my experience shows, you can still succeed with hard work and dedication to break the financial generational curse in your family tree.

This is possible for so many of us. By cultivating financial, business, and legal knowledge, we can begin generating wealth for *ourselves* instead of billionaire employers. We can leave our children the sorts of estates we're used to merely seeing on TV.

For those looking to improve their generational wealth and financial well-being, I offer many services including free mentorship calls to teach you the business, financial, and legal realities that they *don't* teach in schools. Myself and many other Black millionaire mentors can help you to turn your mission, passion, and skills into a fortune.

Let's all get there. Together.

The Sense that Success Lies in Crime

We have all seen the deadly intersection of poverty with the War on Drugs. Even as the government arrests, brutalizes, and incarcerates our young people for their involvement in the drug trade, many of our young people feel that the drug trade is the best or only feasible road to wealth for them as individuals.

As we've already seen, the "school to prison pipeline" is a system of laws and practices designed to deprive Black children of high-quality education and lucrative legal careers, driving them instead toward illegal careers and ultimately incarceration where they may be forced to perform unpaid labor. The legal and financial underpinnings of this system can make it feel impossible to change, but there are actually at least four different fronts on which we can protect our children. These fronts are parenting, financial literacy, entertainment and culture, and political involvement.

One of these fronts is the **involvement of caring, strong, and successful father figures in our children's lives**. When the example of the Black man who is successful in a legal career path exists within the home, the influences of school, media, and racist laws and law enforcement all become secondary.

When this example is absent, on the other hand, children may look to other community figures and media figures for their examples of a well-lived life. In a society permeated by the school-to-prison pipeline, these examples are likely to include the figures glorified in hip hop or what's called "trap music" as well as local drug dealers who have fallen into lives of crime – just as planned by the school-to-prison pipeline.

Later in this book, we'll discuss ways that we can change this narrative by changing our *culture* around business, status, and success. By changing the way we create and consume entertainment and the examples we set for our children, we can completely revolutionize this narrative.

We can teach our children that the paths of President Barack Obama, Samuel L. Jackson, Chris Gardner, Jay-Z, Shaquille O'Neal, and Eddie Murphy are just as open to them as the paths of the drug dealers who they already see glorified as examples of successful Black people in the media.

While we are working together to change our communal culture – an endeavor that is sure to take time – we can change our culture at *home* by making sure that our children have strong, present, and caring father figures who can set the example of triumphing over adversity without falling into the trap of criminal activity and mass incarceration.

Change begins at home. Our immediate family is the *easiest* realm for us to change, because it's directly within our control. By cultivating greater financial success and political involvement in our own lives, we can also change the legal and material realities that can make it so easy for our young people to be lost in the school to prison pipeline.

The Antidote: Becoming a Fatherless Father

My first book, "The Fatherless Father," explores in-depth how my mother and extended family were able to raise me with strong, supportive Black men in my life despite my own father's absence while I was growing up.

At the age of 30 years old, I was able to connect with my biological father for the first time in my life. He is one of my best friends to this day. But for those of us who are raising children without a father involved, how can we help our children to have the confidence, support, and success they need to realize their unlimited potential?

Although we often don't hear about them in popular media, examples abound of successful Black men who have made great contributions to their own communities and attained great wealth and power for themselves by overcoming the financial, cultural, and legal challenges our society presents us with. I want to take a moment to briefly discuss a few of these role models here.

President Barack Obama

Everyone knows who Barack Hussein Obama is. The first Black president of the United States, he himself is a fatherless father.

Although Barack grew up without much involvement from his own dad, who divorced his wife when he was three, he knew that his father studied at Harvard and eventually worked as a senior analyst for the Kenyan government's Ministry of Finance. The stories he heard of his father from his mother and grandparents helped him to form an image of the brilliant and ambitious man who had fathered him.

In so many ways, Barack Obama's biography reads like that of any Black boy or man of today. Though he spent his early years in Indonesia being taught multiple languages and learning life lessons from his Indonesian stepfather, by late elementary school he was back in the American school system where he went by the nickname "Barry." He loved basketball and even dabbled with marijuana with his high school friends.

In his memoir, Obama remembers using drugs and alcohol as a teenager to numb himself to questions about his absent father, and what his own destiny was as a Black teenager living in the United States.

After graduating from high school, "Barry" Obama was awarded a full scholarship to Occidental College in Los Angeles, where he spoke against the actions of the Apartheid government in South Africa. He later transferred to Columbia University, where he majored in political science with a specialty in international relations. He spent a year working at the Business International Corporation as a financial researcher and writer before becoming a project coordinator for the New York Public Interest Research Group.

Obama's background in politics, international relations, finance, and project management all helped make him one of the finest presidents of the last half-century.

As President, he passed unprecedented laws extending more rights to patients and extending healthcare access to tens of millions of Americans. Thanks to him, American insurance companies must allow children to stay on their parents' insurance until the age of 26 (instead of the previous cutoff of age 18), insurance companies are not allowed to refuse people coverage because of pre-existing health conditions, insurance companies must cover *some* preventative care exams, and people who do not have health insurance through their jobs can get it for a fraction of the previous free market price through Healthcare.gov.

As President, Barack Obama also ended the Great Recession – the worst economic downturn America had seen since the 1930s, which began with a catastrophic financial market and job market crash near the end of George W. Bush's term as president. By the time Obama left office, the U.S. was on its way to a budget surplus and had entered what would become the longest continuous spate of economic growth in U.S. history. Through smart stimulus spending and project management, Barack Obama was able to improve the quality of life for all Americans, and especially those who had struggled with unemployment and inability to afford healthcare.

The knowledge of his father's career in the government of his home country of Kenya doubtless helped Barack believe in his own ability to succeed whatever he set his mind to – including obtaining an Ivy League education and becoming involved in first state, then federal politics. His unwavering dedication to fighting systemic racism at home and abroad, and improving the lives of people everywhere, allowed him to accomplish record-breaking achievements that we all continue to benefit from today.

His knowledge of what was possible for his father helped form his understanding of what was possible for him, and ultimately his groundbreaking work as America's first Black president.

LeBron James

LeBron James is a household name for many fans of basketball worldwide. But did you know that he's also the son of a single mom who was 16 when she had him?

As a child, young LeBron was inspired by a local football coach who not only introduced him to basketball, but also acted as a father figure. His mother, Gloria, even allowed young LeBron to move in with the coach, Frank Walker, so he could remain on his football team when his mother moved away from where they were living at the time.

By middle school, LeBron played for the local Amateur Athletic Union team. He and three teammates, who called themselves the "Fab Four," promised to attend high school together and chose to attend a local Catholic school to get the best education available.

While still in high school, LeBron's skill was so great that he began to be featured in national athletic magazines and was awarded the title of Ohio Mr. Basketball. No doubt a tremendous basketball phenom, some sports analysts speculated that LeBron could have played for the National Football League if he'd chosen to focus on football instead of basketball.

Today LeBron James is one of the most celebrated and successful basketball players of all time. At the time of this publication, he is a three time NBA champion, three time NBA Finals Most Valuable Player (MVP), four time NBA MVP, sixteen time NBA All Star, twelve time All-NBA First Team, has won multiple Gold medals representing the United States in the Olympic Games, has been named NBA Rookie of the Year, and has received many other awards and recognitions!

His extreme skill on the basketball court has allowed him to give a voice to players everywhere. When LeBron James speaks, people listen. *Forbes* magazine has long ranked him as one of the world's most influential athletes, and he has been named to Time Magazine's 100 Most Influential People in the World multiple times as well.

Outside of sports, LeBron and his business partner Maverick Carter own their own production company called SpringHill entertainment. They have produced television shows and sports documentaries in conjunction with multiple television networks and major movie studies including Lionsgate, Disney XD, Starz, Showtime, and CNBC. LeBron has announced that he is now working with rapper 2 Chainz on a new album, Rap or Go to the League, which is being created specifically with the intention of "celebrating

Black excellence and focusing on the power of education and entrepreneurship."

As if all that didn't keep him busy enough, LeBron is a financial supporter of After-School All-Stars, the Boys & Girls Club of America, and Children's Defense Fund. He runs his own charity foundation, the LeBron James Family Foundation, and he has donated millions of dollars to the Smithsonian National Museum of African American History and Culture. In 2017 he received the J. Walter Kennedy Citizenship Award from the NBA for his community service, and helped to co-create the "I Promise School," a public elementary school designed to help struggling elementary school students to stay in school. As of 2018, LeBron said he considers this the most important professional accomplishment of his life.

Given his sense of civic duty, it's perhaps not surprising that LeBron has also been outspoken on issues such as the war in Darfur, the murders of Trayvon Martin and Eric Garner, and everyday racism encountered by Black Americans. He has been an outspoken critic of any public figure who makes racist remarks and has stated that "our youth deserve better" than the Trump campaign.

Perhaps fittingly, LeBron James also once gathered over 20,000 people for a viewing of Barack Obama's 30-minute *American Stories, American Solutions* television advertisement, after which Jay-Z held a free concert for attendees. James, Obama, and Jay-Z have been instrumental in modeling what is possible when Black Americans work together for progress and change.

Perhaps most importantly, Lebron James has three children with his high school sweetheart, Savannah, who became his wife after over a decade of dating.

Samuel L. Jackson

Samuel L. Jackson is one of the Internet's favorite celebrities. He is an actor and producer whose films have grossed over $27 billion in ticket sales worldwide and whose sense of humor has helped cement his place in the hearts of billions of fans.

Jackson isn't just a millionaire entertainer. He's also an almost-marine biologist (he obtained his degree in marine biology before becoming an actor), a husband and father, a political activist who has fought for equal rights, and a philanthropist who has donated money to support education for Black children both in the United States and Africa.

Although Samuel L. Jackson met his own father only twice before losing him to alcohol-related health complications, Jackson was supported growing up by his mother, grandparents, and aunts and uncles. The support of strong, caring male family members doubtless helped Jackson to succeed, even overcoming a speech impediment in order to become a great stage performer.

One thing many people don't know about Samuel L. Jackson is that he stuttered as a child, and still sometimes stutters to this day. His list of charitable causes includes The Stuttering Foundation – a group that provides free resources, education, and support to people who stutter and their families.

Chris Gardner

Those of you who have seen the Will Smith movie "The Pursuit of Happyness" already know the story of Chris Gardner. Gardner's only Black male role model in his early years was his abusive stepfather who eventually falsely reported his mother for welfare fraud, resulting in his mother's imprisonment and her children being separated and placed in foster care.

Foster care turned out to have a silver lining: his nuclear family's breakup led to Gardner meeting his uncles, his mother's brothers. With the example of his uncles Archibald, William, and Henry, Gardner had caring, supportive, strong Black men as role models in his life for the first time.

Although his Uncle Henry – a U.S. Navy veteran who became like a father to Gardner – died while young Chris was still a child, his support and positive example doubtless contributed to Gardner's belief that he could do great things as a Black man, and his later unwavering support of his own son even while struggling with homelessness.

Gardner went on to join the Navy, then begin working in clinical research after his discharge. His strong work ethic and quick mind led to his promotion to head of the cardiac surgery research laboratory he worked in, in which capacity he co-authored several papers which were published in medical journals. This is an achievement usually reserved for medical doctors and nurses, but Gardner was able to make important contributions to the field without a medical degree.

Gardner went on to have a son, but hardship struck when changes to the medical industry left Gardner with a salary of just $8,000 – not nearly enough to support his son and live-in girlfriend. He was eventually jailed after over an accrued $1,200 in unpaid parking tickets, which interfered with his career.

His pay dropped even further when he moved into a position which paid only sales commissions – no base salary – and he found himself unable to afford to pay rent. During this time, Gardner's girlfriend left his son in his sole custody, and the two struggled with homelessness together. Gardner and his son were eventually offered a place in a church-run shelter for homeless women after a local pastor became concerned for their safety.

Gardner eventually accrued sufficient savings to start a brokerage firm, Gardner Rich & Co.. There his hard work and intellect paid off again, and the humble firm he first ran out of his small apartment made him millions of dollars over the years to come.

As the money stacked up Gardner quickly turned his attention to philanthropy. He met with Nelson Mandela to discuss how investing could help to improve the wealth and power of Black people in South Africa after the end of Apartheid, and helped to fund a $50 million project to create affordable housing for low-income San Francisco residents like he himself had once been.

Today, Gardner also serves on the board of the National Fatherhood Initiative – a group that promotes responsible fatherhood as a key part of the well-being of children. Doubtless inspired by the influence of father figures in his own life and the responsibility he took for his son, Gardner seeks to ensure that every child has a supportive, caring, strong father in the home. He also serves on the board of the National Education Foundation and uses his own money to sponsor awards for educational assistants who distinguish themselves by providing excellent support for teachers and students alike.

Gardner's story is filled with examples of not only the power of fatherhood, but the power of Black community. The emotional and material support of Gardner's own uncles and the church-run women's shelter allowed Gardner to provide a positive example and a safe, secure living environment for his son. Their support ultimately allowed Gardner to leverage his brilliant mind to create vast wealth, which he then went on to share with Black people in South Africa and children across the United States.

Jay-Z

The rapper Jay-Z was born with the legal name Shawn Carter. He was raised in the housing projects of Brooklyn by a single mother after his father abandoned the family. Though Jay-Z met and reconciled with his father later in life, Jay-Z has spoken of the pain caused by his father's absence in his early years.

Jay-Z loved music from an early age. While he was growing up, his mother and siblings complained that he would wake them up by tapping out beats on the family's furniture in the middle of the night. As he grew, Jay-Z used his musical talent to make a name for himself on the local scene, and was mentored by the rapper and music producer Jaz-O. Jay-Z adopted his stage name to honor Jaz-O, whose support, care, and positive example helped Jay-Z believe in himself and learn skills essential to success in the music industry.

Jay-Z worked his way up from the bottom of the music industry, assisting other rappers and producers with their shows. After procuring his first record deal, he sold CDs out of his car. He soon started his own independent recording label and made a deal with a major music distributor, leading his album *Reasonable Doubt* to hit the Billboard 200 and obtain positive reviews from critics. Today, *Reasonable Doubt* has achieved platinum status and is considered one of the "500 Greatest Albums of All Time" by *Rolling Stone*.

He continued to produce excellent music and make smart business deals for decades after the success of *Reasonable Doubt*. He became a household name both through his music and through merchandising and endorsement deals with companies such as Reebok. In 2002, Jay-Z began his relationship with Beyonce. He was featured in two of Beyonce's hit singles, and the two were featured as *Time Magazine's* "Most Powerful Couple" for the year 2006.

Jay-Z honored the birth of their first child with his moving single "Glory" in 2012. Today Beyonce and Jay-Z have three children together.

Jay-Z runs the Shawn Carter Foundation – an organization that helps students facing financial hardship to pay for college. He has worked with the United Nations to raise awareness about water shortages around the world, and has funded relief efforts in the aftermath of Hurricane Katrina as well as the current fight against police brutality. In 2008, he encouraged voters to go to the polls to vote for President Barack Obama.

According to *Forbes* in June 2019, the Brooklyn-born artist-turned-entrepreneur's business empire was worth $1 **billion**, making him "one of only a handful of entertainers to become a billionaire — and the first hip-hop artist to do so."

Shaquille O'Neal

Shaquille O'Neal grew up without a father after his biological father became addicted to drugs, and was ultimately incarcerated for drug use, while Shaq was still an infant. Though he was cared for by his stepfather, Shaq voiced his feelings of hurt and abandonment by his biological father in his song "Biological Didn't Bother." Shaq reconciled with his father in 2013, years after the song was released. In his conversation with his biological father, Shaq expressed his gratitude for his stepfather's positive example and caring presence in his life.

In addition to his stepfather's care, Shaq has credited the Boys and Girls Club of America with giving him a safe place and positive role models to inspire him to greatness. Shaq helped his team to win the Texas state high school basketball championship after practicing at the Boys and Girls Club's basketball court.

Shaq received numerous accolades for his performance as a college basketball player while he studied for his business degree at Louisiana State University. He was recruited into the NBA and was swiftly named Rookie of the Year before being voted into the All Star game.

For two years, Shaq led the NBA in scoring thanks to his dedication to excellence. He later played on the U.S. Olympic basketball team and finished his career as a four-time NBA Champion, three-time NBA finals MVP, NBA MVP, and fifteen-time NBA All-Star along with several other professional athletic accomplishments.

In addition to his remarkable athletic career, Shaq holds a Bachelor's of Arts in Business, a minor in political science, and a Doctor of Education degree in Human Resource Development. He has stated his intent to further his education by attending law school and becoming a lawyer. He is also a platinum-selling rapper, an actor and voice actor, a businessman, and an investor. Now that's an impressive resume!

Perhaps most importantly of all, Shaq is also a father. He has five children, one of whom earned a place among the nation's top high school basketball players and is now a college basketball player.

Eddie Murphy

Eddie Murphy was born in Brooklyn, New York. His parents broke up when young Murphy was just three years old, and his father was not very involved in his life after the break-up. Eddie Murphy's father died when he was eight years old, leaving Murphy to enter the foster care system when his mother became ill soon after. After one year in foster care, Murphy's mother recovered and the family was reunited. Murphy spent his teenage years with his mother and stepfather.

Murphy knew he wanted to be a comedian from the time he was 15 years old. He learned to impersonate popular singers as well as comedians, and began performing at local clubs while he was still in high school.

In the 1980s, Murphy's superb sense of comedic timing and acting landed him a spot on the cast of Saturday Night Live. Murphy has been ranked as the second most important SNL performer of all time. Some have credited him with keeping the show alive with his beloved and hysterical characters during a five-year period of internal crisis when the show's direction and production suffered.

Murphy went on to a career in Hollywood, starring in numerous films throughout the 1980s, 1990s, and 2000s. He is also a musician who has produced multiple albums and collaborated with artists including the Bus Boys, Michael Jackson, and Snoop Dogg.

Like the other men on this list, Eddie Murphy is a father himself despite struggling with abandonment by father figures early in his life. He has three children, the youngest of whom is named for his brother who died of leukemia in 2017.

Like the other Black millionaires on this list, Murphy has engaged in philanthropy to lift up the Black community and people everywhere. He has financially supported the AIDS Healthcare Foundation, the Martin Luther King, Jr. Center, and the relief fund for the Screen Actors' Guild strike. He has also donated money to causes including cancer, education, the creative arts, family support, healthcare, and homeless charities.

The Next Step

A better future for the Black community starts at home. It starts with giving our children caring, strong, and committed mother *and* father figures who *show* them that greatness is possible for them.

Home is where the heart is, and it's where all true change begins. Even though not all relationships and or marriages work out, it doesn't have to mean a broken family connection for the child.

Responsibly co-parenting and showing the child how to successfully manage any adversity will serve the child well. If the child doesn't have a father present in the home, like I didn't, it's strongly advised for the mother or parental guardian to provide the child access to a strong male figure. This man can model what a strong Black man looks like, whether directly or indirectly.

There are several mentorship programs offered across the country that can help. My book "The Fatherless Father" was written to assist single mothers and their children with these challenges, and to assist grown men who grew up fatherless and who may still deal with unspoken pain.

In addition to providing strong father figures and family relationships, we must provide ourselves and our children with the financial literacy we need to build the kind of wealth that can change our family history for generations to come.

Chapter 3

Financial Education:
The Foundation of Generational Change

"Intelligence can create huge profits, and in fact, you can actually make more money being smart than you can be strong or fast."

- Robert F. Smith

The statistics on financial inequality in America can be shocking. As of 2020, the average net worth of a white family was roughly *ten times* the average net worth of a Black family: $171,000 to $17,150. Needless to say, this makes a huge difference to the kind of education and jobs that are available to future generations of Black families.

When you start out in an underfunded school district without the ability to afford private schools, it can be hard to get ahead in life. But it might surprise you to learn that the biggest determinant of financial success is often *not* education or school tuition: it's financial literacy and entrepreneurial skills which are *not* taught in schools.

Despite Robert Kiyosaki's current political views and recent social media posts that disturb many, including myself, his first book changed many lives, including mine. One of the best-selling financial literacy books of all time, "Rich Dad, Poor Dad" discusses the financial skills that low-income fathers often can't teach their kids – because they were never taught these skills themselves.

It turns out there's a whole set of skills, laws, rules, tips, and tricks for growing wealth that wealthy families teach their kids, but *don't* incorporate into school curricula. And there's even more: entrepreneurship is *also* not typically taught in schools – at least not effectively – and it is often the key to generating truly massive amounts of wealth without even requiring a college degree.

Ever wonder why some of the world's wealthiest, most successful people didn't even finish college? Bill Gates and Steve Jobs became rich, not because they had Ivy League educations, but because they had the vision to create and sell a product the world hadn't yet realized it needed.

Though the road to success often *does* lead through the Ivy League – some of America's Black billionaires of today earned their place using skills and knowledge learned in science, technology, engineering, math, and business skills – it turns out that it's what a child learns *at home* that makes the biggest difference in their financial security and success.

It's not hard to see *why* so much inequality exists between Black and white families. As we've covered in previous chapters, Black Americans have often been legally prevented from owning property, living in the best school districts, being hired into the best job titles, or claiming the full value of the labor of their own hands for most of American history.

To this day, white men are favored above all other groups in the most lucrative fields in America: those of science, medicine, business, finance, and law. This infuriating continued discrimination has been proven using double-blind resume studies – studies where identical resumes with different names are sent to employers.

When asked to rate each resume on a scores such as competence, qualification, and hireability, employers in all of these fields rated *the same resumes* higher on average across all fields when the names and extracurriculars listed on them implied that the resumes belonged to white men. A Scott Johnson was rated as more qualified and more likely to be hired than a Jamal Jackson by business and finance firms, legal firms, and scientific laboratories, even when both had identical qualifications and experience.

Some have argued that Black people and women enjoy "reverse discrimination" in that the same studies found that Black and female names were more likely to be hired in the fields of art, literature, and childcare. But this "reverse discrimination" starts to look like plain old ordinary discrimination when one discovers that these are all among the *lowest-paying* professional fields in the country.

With employers continuing to favor white employees for their highest-paying job titles and Black employees for their lowest-paying work, it can feel tempting to give up and say there's nothing we can do. But nothing could be further from the truth. The truth is that financial literacy and entrepreneurship skills can allow you to *build* wealth, even if traditional employers are hesitant to give you a chance.

It's helpful to know the situation we're facing: that as Black people, we may have to learn *more* skills to gain equal acceptance by white-dominated financial establishments. But it's just as helpful to know that Black people throughout history have built wealth despite all of the obstacles in their path, and we can easily do the same.

In the previous chapter we discussed the importance of positive role models, so let's take a look at some successful instances of Black people building extreme wealth in American history. These paths to success provide roadmaps that we can all follow.

We're not going to discuss the paths of popular entertainers and athletes here, because most of us already know their stories. It's also worth noting that "athlete" and "entertainer" are actually among the *lowest*-paying industries in America, on average. While the best of the best in these industries can become billionaires of incredible influence and wealth, most people who pursue those paths instead find themselves as starving artists, or trapped in a less-than-ideal fallback career.

There's nothing wrong with those paths, to be clear. But they aren't how white Americans built most of their wealth. To see how the drastic wealth differences between the Black and white communities arose, we must look at how we can encourage our children to walk the paths of business, finance, law, science, technology, and math.

Freedman's Savings & Trust

After the abolition of slavery, Freedman's Savings & Trust became the first bank dedicated to working for Black Americans, by Black Americans. Its business model – accepting cash deposits from freed slaves and using the pooled money to allow its members to procure legal services, business loans, and other essential services – was a runaway success at first.

The bank soon accrued hundreds of thousands of dollars in collective resources. Since this was 150 years ago, we can go ahead and add a couple of decimals to that figure to account for inflation. In other words, these freed slaves had soon accrued *tens of millions of dollars* in assets, which they planned to use to continue building their businesses and communities.

Unfortunately, unequal treatment soon decimated this bank. When Congress decided to exempt Freedman's Savings & Trust from national banking regulations – regulations designed to prevent catastrophic crashes, which white banks were required to abide by – Freedman's Savings & Trust was soon hemorrhaging money. Cursed by unequal treatment and mismanagement by the government, the bank lost the assets its constituents had deposited and closed its doors in 1874.

The Tulsa Greenwood District

The Tulsa Greenwood district was made possible by the acquisition of some of the very first land not owned by whites in the post-slavery South. The land was technically given out under the Dawes Act, which broke up communally owned American Indian lands into individual family allotments.

How did this result in the rise of a thriving Black community? Well, the American Indians thought much more highly of Black people than Southern whites did at the time. In fact, although some American Indian tribes had owned slaves, many also welcomed escaped slaves as full-fledged members of their societies. As a result, Black former slaves and their children were among the American Indians who received land under the Dawes Act.

The Black-owned land in Texas became an instant sanctuary for Black families for decades to come. Attracted by the rare prospect of living in an autonomous Black community, Black communities founded more than 50 townships across Texas and began to purchase additional swaths of land with their newly-earned wealth to expand their communities.

By 1906, the wealthy Black landowner O. W. Gurley was giving out loans to Black people who came to the Greenwood district with plans to start their own businesses. This investment capital grew rapidly as Greenwood's residents mastered the skills of business and finance, and Greenwood soon boasted the largest Black-owned hotel in the country and its own Black-run newspaper which covered matters of legal, political, and financial importance to its still newly-free Black population.

Greenwood had its own school district, hospital, savings and loan bank, and bus and taxi service. Its wealth was so admired that it soon came to be envied – and white violence led to Greenwood's downfall.

In the early 20th century, the Ku Klux Klan began to experience a resurgence. Preying on the financial anxiety of white Southerners, racist agitators blamed Southern Blacks for all of the hardships experienced by Southern whites. Greenwood was portrayed by some agitators as proof of the "theft" of white wealth – that is, wealth created by Black hands that whites felt entitled to own.

The *Tulsa Star* encouraged Greenwood residents to arm themselves in response to potential white threats. It went so far as encouraging armed Black people to stand guard near courthouses and jails so that fellow Blacks tried and incarcerated under racist laws would not be lynched or die in police custody.

Eventually, the spark of armed confrontation between Greenwood's residents and resentful whites was an accusation of sexual assault of a white woman against a Greenwood resident. When it became clear that lynching was a real danger, 25 armed Black veterans arrived to the courthouse to volunteer to guard the accused man. The crowd eventually swelled to 75 armed Black people who were anxious about their safety and the safety of their neighbors.

Terrified by what they saw as the threat of "armed, violent Black folks," over 1,500 white people descended on Greenwood, destroying property, looting homes, and shooting residents.

Though other Black townships and organizations such as the NAACP offered legal and financial help, the damage to Greenwood was too great. Much of the wealth built up over the previous decades was lost.

Robert F. Smith

Robert F. Smith is a scientist, businessman, and billionaire. As a child his parents brought him to the March on Washington, where Martin Luther King, Jr. delivered his famous "I have a dream" speech.

It's certain that the example of his parents and of Martin Luther King, Jr. assisted Smith in obtaining an internship at Bell Labs. Though he was initially denied the internship, being told he was too young for it, Smith called the Massachusetts Institute of Technology on a weekly basis until the laboratory, impressed by his persistence, gave him the internship when a less dedicated MIT student did not show up to work.

Smith went on to become a chemical engineer for several major technology companies, and then a banking and investment advisor for Goldman Sachs and Silicon Valley tech firms. In 2000 he founded his own venture capital firm, Vista Equity Partners which now controls over $50 billion in assets.

Smith has become the first Black man to serve as board chairman for Carnegie Hall and the Robert F. Kennedy Human Rights organization. He serves on the board for Cornell Engineering College, the Columbia Business School, and the Boys and Girls Club of San Francisco.

Robert F. Smith was the largest single donor of funds to the City of Hope gala in 2018, where he donated millions to research specifically directed toward studying treatments for strains of breast cancer and prostate cancer for Black women and men.

You may have heard of the speaker that did the commencement address at Morehouse College in 2019 that paid the student loan debt off for the entire graduating class, yep, that was him. Robert Smith.

Smith's belief that he could succeed in science and technology and his mastery of business and financial skills combined to allow him to become a billionaire, and invest his wealth in the health of Black Americans everywhere.

Any of our children may follow his example, if they grow up with sufficient faith in their abilities in both science and technology *and* business and finance.

David Steward

David Steward was born to a mechanic and a stay-at-home mom in Chicago, Illinois. He spent much of his life in Clinton, Missouri, where he grew up in impoverished neighborhoods and faced segregation. Steward grew up in the era of racially segregated schools and movie theaters, when Black people were not allowed to swim in the local public swimming pool.

Despite hearing from society that he was not enough, his parents' supportive example assisted him in obtaining his Bachelor's of Science in Business and working his way up from salesman to senior account executive at Federal Express. After being named Salesman of the Year, he owned and founded several businesses which have together made him a billionaire.

While Robert F. Smith used science and technology expertise to spot great investment opportunities, David Steward used people skills and street smarts in addition to his formal business education to become a billion-dollar salesman and entrepreneur.

Today, his company World Wide Technologies controls over $11 billion and is one of the largest companies based in St. Louis, Missouri. He is the coauthor of "Doing Business by the Good Book," a book about conducting business and finance in accordance with Biblical principles.

David Steward shows us by example that it's possible to accumulate vast wealth for our families and communities without compromising our moral values.

Any of our children may follow in his footsteps if they combine their street smarts and people skills with personal development and knowledge of the worlds of business and finance.

The Plan for Generational Wealth

Now that we've seen how past Black communities and individuals have succeeded in building generational wealth – even if some of it was lost to racist actions – we can start to think about a blueprint for how we as individuals and communities can build this same kind of wealth on an even larger scale.

What is it that the wealthy fathers of "Rich Dad, Poor Dad" were able to teach their kids that the low-income fathers were never taught? I highly recommend reading Kiyosaki's book to get a broader take, but the most important knowledge for financial literacy, in my experience, has been this:

#1 – *Identify Your Position*

Before you know how to get to your destination, you have to know your current location. So where do you stand financially, right now?

You cannot correct what you are not willing to confront. That's so important, I'm going to say it again:

You cannot correct what you are not willing to confront.

Many of us go through life not wanting to think too hard about our financial situation. As long as we've got a roof over our heads, we're golden. Right? But as we've seen in the preceding chapters, just having a roof doesn't get your kids into the best schools or the best career opportunities. It doesn't build wealth that you can use to lift up your community.

The good news is, *every single one of us* can improve our financial situation. Even without getting a new job. It's true. These are the secret skills that rich folks teach their children, which most of our parents had no opportunity to learn.

If you can never get out of debt, maybe it's not because it's impossible – you simply don't know how.

Maybe you don't even realize that there are secret skills out there that rich people – people whose families are rich for *generations* – use to grow their wealth. That's the boat most of us are in: since these skills aren't taught in schools, most of us have no clue they even exist.

Maybe you feel that these secret skills are too hard to live by, or that you shouldn't have to bother. That's certainly a choice you're free to make, but I'll tell you what that choice *won't* do: it won't help you become rich or put your kids on the road to generational wealth.

So what is it going to be? Are you going to keep letting things be "just the way it is," or are you going to take some of the steps we're about to talk about to change your life, and your kids' lives, for the better?

This isn't about your financial self-image, or your "gut feeling" about how much money you have or where you feel you are right now. This isn't about how much you make compared to your neighbors, or your own parents. This is about cold, hard numbers. The kinds of numbers that finance wizards work with to create millions. The numbers you need to know include:

What is your income? After taxes and benefits, what is the take-home pay that you get to keep to pay your bills and build your savings and your wealth?

Remember, getting serious in the finance game means thinking about the *future* before we think about the present. When we get more money, if we want to build generational wealth, we don't spend it. Instead we *save* it or *invest* it in paying off debts, buying stocks and bonds, and other outlets that will give you *more money back than you put in* in the future.

How much do you have in savings? Letting money sit there in the bank can feel boring, but it can be crucial if any surprises occur. Having savings in the bank can be the difference between becoming homeless or not during job loss or a medical emergency. And if nothing bad happens, savings can be used for a variety of things that we will discuss later.

What are your debts? Most of us have some form of debt, whether they're from credit cards, mortgages, student loans, or something else. Now the important thing about debt is that most debts *charge interest* – meaning that if you don't pay them off right away, you get charged even more money just for letting that debt sit there unpaid.

So let's create a plan to reduce and pay off our debts as quickly as possible. No reason to get charged interest when we get no value in return.

What is your credit score? Remember, you actually have *three* credit scores that are primarily used by creditors that are reported by three major credit bureaus: Equifax, Experian, and Transunion. These three *usually* roughly agree, but sometimes they might be slightly different. Credit bureaus can even make mistakes with your credit, like reporting your bill payments wrong or putting the wrong person's information on your account. If there's incorrect information on your account, you can file a petition to fix it or get a company to help you – but only if you know that there's been a mistake in the first place.

That's why it's crucial to learn *all three* of your credit scores, and monitor them regularly. Credit scores often determine whether you can buy property, buy cars, or obtain business loans from the bank, so keeping them in good shape is *crucial* to building generational wealth. You may even be required to pay higher rates on homes, cars, and other loans if your credit score is low, and offered lower rates and prices if your credit score is high.

What do your investments look like? If you don't have any, that's a new financial goal! Money invested wisely into stocks and bonds grows a lot faster than money in your savings account or under your mattress, so investing is a major goal to build generational wealth.

What is your plan to enhance *all of these numbers?*

I encourage you to stop reading for a minute right now. Get on your computer and figure out what *all* of those numbers are for you.

Then make a quick plan, as best you can, for how to improve every single one of them. Just a little. Over time. One day at a time. One week at a time. Month. Year. And boom, you're there! Your financial situation is changed forever!

Improving your income: are there new skills you could learn that could get you promoted, or qualify you to work for an employer who pays more? Look up what the hottest certifications and skills are in your field. I'll bet there's something you can learn in the next three months.

Improving your savings: plan to put a little extra into savings each month. It can be just $50, and it can come out of your party money. This might sound boring, but guess what? If you deposit $50 a month for a year, you will have *$600* in emergency funds at the end of the year. If that means you can afford a repair or a bill without taking out a high-interest loan, you'll end up with more money than you put in.

Improving your debt: pay, pay, pay. See if you can find another $50 somewhere in your budget to put toward your debt with the highest interest rate. Don't know the interest rates on your debts? Look it up! If you've got one that's charging 7% and one that's charging 3.5%, you'll save twice as much by paying off the 7% debt first.

Improve your credit scores. This can be as simple as using your credit card less, paying off your credit card bills on time, or in some cases using your credit cards *more* if you're someone with no credit history. Remember: never take out a credit card because you want to spend more money. That's not rich people thinking.

Instead, take out a credit card because you want to build your credit history. Charge no more than 10-20% of your credit limit to it per month, and then pay it off immediately. This proves that you pay your bills without depleting your bank account. Lastly, look at your credit report and create a plan to correct items that are negatively impacting your credit score. We will discuss this more later in this chapter.

Improve your investments. Don't have any investments? Get some! Choosing an investment can require some expertise, but it can pay off big time. Investment portfolios can more than double in value over the course of a few decades – meaning that if you put $10,000 in, you can get $20,000 out when it's time for the kids to inherit your wealth. We'll talk more about how to play this game, and learn to play it right, later in this chapter.

If building generational wealth and a better future for your children is on your to-do list, pay attention to the financial skills coming at us in the sections to come and start *putting them into action in your life.*

There are at least a few things you can start doing *today* to improve your financial situation. I promise.

At first, you might actually find that your spending money decreases in the short term. When you're putting money into paying off debts and making investments in the short term, you might have less to spend on short-term luxury items.

But you know what? All of that money you're putting into paying debts and making investments *now* is money that is being magnified. It's money that is saving you from paying interest payments to rich folks, and even requiring the rich folks to pay capital gains to *you* when you invest your money in becoming part owner of their corporations.

Sounds like a pretty sweet deal, right? We'll discuss more of how to go about paying off debts, investing, and acquiring other sources of generational wealth in the sections to come.

#2 – Budget and Plan

You might be thinking the above ideas sound great, but you're not sure where the money is going to come from. That's where this next step comes in handy.

I encourage you to take a moment, right now if you can, to print out your bank statements from the last few months. Try to print out a statement that lists every single transaction you've had – every time you've been paid or spent money – going back three months.

Now, I want you to get two different colored highlighters or markers. Pick one color for your "necessary spending" – spending that you absolutely can't do without, such as rent bills, health insurance, electric bills, etc.. Use the other color for "unnecessary spending" – things you can cut without getting into trouble, such as money spent on parties, luxury items, and entertainment.

Don't worry – we're not going to ask you to give up *all* your unnecessary spending. But you might be shocked when you realize how much you could be putting into savings, paying off debts, and investments – all actions that will build generational wealth and *give you more money in the long run than you're earning right now* – once you've added up all the spending you don't actually need to live.

You might find yourself asking some questions about how much you really want that restaurant food vs. how much you want to build financial freedom and power over time.

Now that you've got your essentials vs. your non-essentials listed out, we're going to decide how much you get paid.

#3 – Pay Yourself First

Put your name at the top of your budget list. How much do *you* get paid? How much money goes toward your savings, paying off your debts, and making your investments.

Thinking of this as *paying yourself*. If you are paying *other people* – rent, car note, credit cards, restaurants, cell phone company, etc. – instead of yourself, that's money that *you* don't have in your pocket.

So decide how much you pay *yourself* – not other people – before you do anything else. How fast do you want to build your net worth, financial security, and power?

This is called "asset allocation." It shows you that you're worth it.

Now, you might be asking, what if I can't even pay my bills? How can I possibly even get started with this?

Well, maybe all you can afford to pay yourself is $5. But that $5 is the number you can watch – the number that builds your power and freedom, instead of going to pay other people. That $5 is the number you can expand as you work on all the other steps in this program.

When you prioritize paying *yourself*, you start to realize that you're #1. You've got to be working for yourself and your family *first*.

I recommend that you split your payments to yourself between two savings accounts to start out with.

The first is your **mini-emergency fund**. You want to make sure that your emergency fund has at least **$3,000** in it. This is money that can be used to pay rent, pay a medical bill, or fix a car if something goes wrong. When you have this money, you *won't* need to take out high-interest loans or risk immediate homelessness if you lose your job.

Pay this fund first when you get your paycheck each month. Even if it's only $5 a month at first, depositing that $5 will instill in you the importance of working for *yourself*.

Your *true* **emergency fund** should have at least 6 months worth of your necessary expenses in it. How do you know what your necessary expenses are?

Remember that budget exercise we did earlier? What was the total value of your *necessary* bills? That's your rent, your health insurance, your car payment – anything you can't do without paying each month.

Now, multiply that by six.

That's probably a pretty big number. Hypothetically, let's say your necessary expenses are about $2,000 per month. You want $12,000 in your true emergency fund.

Why? To be safe. When something bad happens, we like to hope that we can be back to work in a few weeks or months. But what if that isn't the case? Having six months worth of savings in the bank gives us time to figure out what to do if that happens.

Sound impossible? I promise it's not. We're going to keep talking about how to do that in the pages to come.

Think about how much peace of mind that would give you.

Once your emergency funds are locked down, I recommend that you also save money for *opportunities*. This is money that you don't need to ensure your basic financial security. It's money you can use to invest in your business – or to have *fun*.

I do recommend that you have a **"fun fund."** What does "fun" mean? Well, whatever it means to you! Maybe it means splurging on a fancy restaurant every once in a while. Maybe it even means a vacation. When you save money for that purpose, you can spend it without guilt. Treat yourself every once in a while.

The final type of fund you want to cultivate is a **fund for your future**.

There are many ways to do this. *After* your emergencies are covered and your ability to take advantage of opportunities, you can start thinking about investing in stocks and bonds that may multiply your money many times over the course of several decades.

I want to make sure that you have a plan for your money. If you don't, even a six-figure paycheck won't ensure that you can retire comfortably, send your kids to college, or buy and keep your dream home. I know people who were millionaires in their 30s or 40s who are selling cars to get by in their 50s and 60s. Why? Not because they couldn't get enough money, obviously. But because they *didn't have a plan for it*. They paid it all to other people for short-term luxuries, racked up debts, and didn't save or invest.

I don't want that to happen to you. Even if you're an average median wage worker, you can build up an impressive amount of wealth by being smart with your money. And even if you're a billionaire superstar – you can find a way to go broke if you assume the money will never stop coming.

This game isn't about how much you get paid right now. It's about how *smart* and *proactive* you are in planning for your future.

Let's prove it.

I'd like you to join me for a quick exercise. Look at your income and your budget. See what happens if you cut *all unnecessary spending* and divide it between your emergency funds.

If you did that, how fast would you meet your emergency fund goals?

See? Just like that you're on track to have more financial security and power than you ever thought before.

Whatever you do, I want you to *start paying yourself first*. This means that when you get paid, you put money into your own savings account – your own fund for your future – *before* you pay anybody else including your landlord, your entertainers, and any other expenses you might have.

If you're not paying yourself, then what benefit are you getting from your labor? If you're not building up a fund for your future, then how will you ever have any power or freedom?

Working full-time and having nothing left in your bank account at the end of the day is similar to working without pay. Even though you're technically getting a paycheck, you're immediately paying all of that money to other people. Whether it's your landlord or your local restaurants, the bottom line is that you have nothing left at the end of the day. You have no money in the bank, and money is power.

What do we call it when someone works without pay? We call it slavery. If you're working full-time only to have nothing left in the bank at the end of the month, this is what some people call "wage slavery." You are technically being paid a wage, but you are being left with nothing after paying your living expenses.

When you start paying yourself first – even if it's just $5 – what you're saying is "enough is enough."

You may be getting a paycheck, but it's all immediately being taken from you. That $5 that you put in your savings account is your commitment to gain your freedom. It's your commitment to take control, and start building wealth.

Now, it might very well be that you need to find a way to make more money, *as well as* finding a way to spend less money. The quickest way to wealth is to reduce your spending *and* increase your income at the same time. Some people teach that you can do one OR the other, but I suggest both!

We'll talk about some ways to increase your income later – but that income won't do you any good if you're paying it all to other people instead of to yourself.

Lastly, below is a plan to show you how to budget and allocate your monthly income. Establishing a plan will help make the success of your financial future more viable.

I want to note here that this income allocation refers to your *after-tax* income.

For most people who are paid a wage or a salary, the money you get from your employer has already been taxed. Your employer pays the taxes before they pay you.

However, if you are self-employed or work as an independent contractor instead of an employee, you may be responsible for paying your own taxes out of your paycheck. If you start your own business, begin working as a freelancer, or begin earning other income that does *not* come from an employer-employee relationship, ensure you read up on what taxes you may owe and pay them *first* to avoid ending up deep in debt to the IRS. If you are unsure how much you owe in taxes as a self-employed individual or independent contractor, you may wish to consult a tax professional or subscribe to a tax software for self-employed individuals.

After your taxes are paid, your ideal income allocation for what is left looks like this:

Monthly Income Allocation:

25% – Housing; no matter if you own or rent
20% – Necessary household bills
10% – Food; home or eating out
10% – Investments
10% – Savings
10% – Tithing & or Charity
 5% – Fun and social activities

5% – Vacations or Travel

5% – Auto loans; never lease, unless for tax advantages

If you are able to use this framework to budget your spending, you can really provide more financial structure to your life and get more of the goals you have accomplished. Feel free to arrange some of the percentages to fit your lifestyle but a plan is necessary for success!

#4 – *Eliminate Your Debt*

It's time for another exercise. Find yourself a debt elimination software – there are many companies that offer these, including my company Novae – and let's find out just exactly how much your debts are costing you.

Remember, debts charge interest. That means you're almost always paying *more than you originally spent or borrowed* back in return for the time you're taking to pay. Debt elimination software can help you input the amounts of your debts, their minimum monthly payments, and their interest rates to determine how much you're actually paying off over time.

If you're not sure how much your interest rates are, that information should appear on your monthly statements or your online account. Remember, always pay off the debts with the highest interest rates first.

Once your highest interest rate debt is paid off, remember to immediately allocate *that same monthly payment* to paying off your other debts. In that way, you can become debt free as soon as possible.

Cash flow is king. Cash flow is the amount of money you have *after* you pay off your bills – so the faster you pay off your debts, the faster you can grow your money and the more money you can have left over for *fun and investing into the future you desire.*

#5 – *Split Your Payments*

To implement these best practices, it's worth noting that there's a clause to look out for in many loans and agreements. Make sure that any agreements you sign *don't* contain penalties for early payoffs. These clauses are known as "early payoff penalties."

Now that might sound like a crazy idea. Why would someone punish you for giving them money *faster?* Well, because they don't get to charge you as much interest if you do that. Because interest charges you more money over time, many companies make their profit projections *assuming* it will take you the standard amount of time – a year, ten years, twenty years – to pay off that loan. If you manage to pay it off much faster, they lose a significant amount of interest. So some companies will try to charge you *extra* for paying your loans off early.

You see the logic now? Everyone's competing for money, and many people don't look close enough at their interest rates, agreement terms, or other documents to realize how to keep more money for themselves.

Now, assuming you've got a major payment plan that *doesn't* contain penalties for early payment, here's what you're going to do: split your payments into two.

Instead of making payments on your mortgage once a month, for example, you're going to split your payment into two. If your mortgage monthly minimum is $1,000, you're going to pay $500 every two weeks.

Note: that's *every two weeks*. Not on the 1st and the 15th, but every other Friday. Why? Because your goal is to get this paid off as fast as possible. And the faster you pay – even the difference between paying at the end of the month, or the few days each month you gain from paying every 14 days instead of every 15 or 16 – all of that reduces the amount of interest that you end up paying.

Paying every two weeks instead of once or twice a month, for example, essentially adds an extra monthly payment each year. This can leave you paying off a 30-year mortgage in 23 years, saving your future self and family tens or hundreds of thousands of dollars. You've essentially just given yourself a massive discount on your home.

Wouldn't you rather have that interest money in your "fun fund" or your investment accounts instead?

If you don't believe in the power of accelerated payments, try using an amortization calculator or asking your financial professional for your amortization schedule. Amortization describes the *total* amount you end up paying over the lifetime of a home or mortgage – principal *plus* interest.

Just take a look and see how much less you'll be paying in total for your home, car, or other loans if you use the every-two-weeks payment schedule instead of paying monthly. You might even look to see what would happen if you could find a way to pay your mortgage *twice* as fast as the bank requires.

How much would you save? What could you do with that money? If you invested it in multiple real estate properties or stock that multiplied its value over the course of 50 years, how much money would you have *then*?

This is how rich people think. This is what they teach their kids that they don't teach in public schools. And this is how they get – and stay – so wealthy that our politicians have to do what they say.

We can do it, too.

I encourage you to call your mortgage company *tomorrow* and tell them that you want to start paying every two weeks, instead of once per month. They may even allow you to...

#6 – *Set It and Forget It*

How much money have you paid on late fees for your bills in the last year? Were your payments late because you didn't have the money – or because you just forgot to make them?

Of course, this requires that you make a budget and stick to it each month. Forgetting about a major autopay withdrawal and overspending is only a problem if you didn't create a monthly budget, or if you didn't stick to it.

This is where all of these skills, from the most basic to the most advanced, come together. If you master budgeting and planning, you can build wealth and live your life with ease.

Some companies appreciate the reliability of autopay income so much, they may even offer discounts or lower interest rates for accounts that are set to autopay.

The best part of "Set It and Forget It?" Instead of being distracted by thinking about and handling the bills, I could dedicate 100% of my brain to making more money. And little improvements in efficiency and stress reduction like that – just like paying your mortgage twice monthly, that extra brain space adds up to seriously increase your earning potential over time.

#7 – Get a Credit Plan

Remember how we mentioned earlier the effects of a good or bad credit score? How people with lower credit scores may be charged higher prices, higher interest rates, or even denied ownership or loans altogether? Well, the reverse is also true. If you can repair your credit – something that anybody can do with proper research and planning – you can lower the prices you're charged, the interest rates you're charged, and even become eligible for loans and property you might otherwise be denied.

Like everything else on this list, this requires planning. You can't just fix it tomorrow: just like anything else that needs restoring, it takes time and a game plan.

My company offers assistance for people seeking to improve their credit situation. We help individuals to analyze and optimize their credit scores through education, software, and services; correcting future behaviors; and leveraging the Fair Credit Reporting Act by asking the credit bureaus to remove negative information on your credit report that cannot be validated. We even show you how to do everything yourself, if you study the materials we offer. This will be one of the most important decisions of your life.

What if you don't have *any* credit? What if you've never had a credit card or taken out a loan?

You might think that's good. On the surface, that makes sense. If you've never spent more money than you've had on hand, that shows that you're a responsible spender. Right?

Well, that's not quite how banks and landlords see it. To them, people with no history of paying back loans or paying off debts haven't proven that they are *capable* of doing those things. To them, lending somebody money who has no credit history might be like putting some random guy up to quarterback who's never held a football before based on the logic that he's never *lost* a game in his life. He may not have any losses on his record, but he doesn't have any wins either.

So how do you rack up wins? You open accounts. But I'm going to repeat my earlier caution: be careful.

Credit card companies *want* you to borrow more than you can pay back. That's because when you do that, they get to charge you interest and late fees. So they won't necessarily encourage you to be responsible and behave in a way that builds positive credit.

When using credit cards to build a credit history, make sure you charge *something* on them each month. But make sure it's something small: the best credit scores go to those who maintain a balance less than 7% of their credit limit each month. And make sure you pay it off completely, every single month. On autopay, if possible.

Those with a history of low credit usage, with high credit limits, and complete, on-time payments are the best candidates for lower prices, lower interest rates, and better products and loans. They've proven that they can pay back loans *and* that they don't spend more money than they've got.

A record of doing that every single month is like a quarterback with a record of winning every single game. And the more games you've got under your belt – or the more months of paying off credit cards in that way – the more impressive the undefeated record becomes.

One way to build up a great credit record *real* fast is to see if a friend or family member with an excellent credit score is comfortable adding you to one of their credit card accounts.

Adding a new user to an account is always a risk for the primary account holder. If you go use that credit card to make purchases you can't pay for, the primary account holder takes a big hit to *their* credit history.

But if you simply get your name added to the account and refrain from using the credit yourself, you effectively gain the good credit history associated with that account. Accounts are measured by amount of years open, not by when an *individual* was added to the account – so you can gain several years of excellent credit history by being added to a friend or family member's account. This can instantly put you in a bracket for better prices, better interest rates, and better purchases.

To build your credit fast and effectively, I recommend a mix of *both* taking out your own credit cards and paying them like the all star described above, and being added to the accounts of friends or family members with excellent accounts. Owning your own credit accounts will also provide you with an additional emergency lifeline in case your emergency savings funds aren't quite full yet.

When you act with planning and intention, you can win. No matter what life throws at you. If you are struggling to believe that you can win, I invite you to become part of the community that attends our free LIVE mentorship calls through Novae weekly.

That's right, we offer you free mentorship from very successful people. It's a community of people who support each other, and who can show you by example that you can win whatever you're going through now.

You can also find multiple mentorship and inspirational mp3s, on several topics, on our website at NovaeMoney.com.

#8 – *Communicate With Your Creditors*

Did you know that you can actually negotiate with creditors and debt collectors? No one tells you that of course, because those companies want to charge you as many late fees, interest payments, and such as possible.

But there's a secret: "distressed debt" – debt that is overdue on repayment – stands a good chance of not getting paid *at all*. Creditors know that, and so they're often willing to work with people who reach out and promise to pay them – and they may do you a favor to encourage you to pay up.

You can actually ask your creditors to list your account as "paid as agreed." This account status effectively erases any red marks on your account for previous missed payments. At the end of the day, after all, why does the company care about putting red marks on your credit score? Their only goal in doing so is to get you to pay them, so if you promise to do that – on the condition that they remove the red marks from your credit score – why wouldn't they do it?

The script goes something like this:

"Hey, I'm <your name here> and I have an outstanding balance of X amount of money. I'd fallen on some hard times, but things are bouncing back now. I'm prepared to pay you Y amount of money (as much as you can manage – remember, eliminating debt saves you interest and late fees), but here is what I need from you. If I pay you

Y amount, I'd like you to update my account status to 'paid as agreed' with the major credit bureaus."

Here's another important secret of the finance world: *always get every agreement in writing.* It doesn't have to be a fancy contract, but even an email documenting your agreement can serve as evidence of your agreement in ways that a spoken conversation cannot. That's why I always send "confirmation emails" to anyone I have an important conversation with. By re-capping what we talked about in writing and obtaining their written agreement to it, I now have written documentation that this conversation happened.

So inform the creditor that you will begin submitting payments *as soon as you receive a letter or e-mail* documenting their promise to update your account status to "paid as agreed."

Even if you're not behind on your payments, you can still call up your credit card companies and other creditors and *negotiate for a better interest rate.*

Here's a script to use for that:

"Hi, I'm <your name here> and I've been an account holder for <X> years. (You don't really have to include the years, but they always want to keep long-time faithful customers.) I've been considering transferring my balance to another provider that offers better interest rates, but I really like your service and would like to stay with you. Is there any way you can offer me a better interest rate?"

Now, that might sound absurd. Why would a company just *give* you a better interest rate? Well, if you're considering moving to another provider, they have a choice between doing that or *losing the ability to charge you interest altogether.*

You can use the same technique to ask them to increase your credit limit:

"I'm thinking about making some major purchases in the future, and some other providers are offering me cards with higher credit limits. Would it be possible for you to increase my current credit limit?"

Again, the provider has a choice here: they can say "yes" and increase your credit limit for free, or they can risk losing any interest they might otherwise have gotten on paying off your major purchase.

Now, *don't use your higher credit limit to spend more money.* Instead, this higher credit limit serves two purposes:

1. It can serve as an emergency credit line in case something happens and your emergency funds aren't full yet.

2. As I mentioned earlier, it lowers your credit utilization – that is, it helps you to use less than 7% of your total credit limit each month – and helps you to look your best for future lenders, banks, etc. and build your credit score the fastest.

   By raising your limit, you're automatically lowering your utilization percentage – $100 of monthly credit utilization might be 10% of a card with a $1,000 limit, but it's only 5% of a card with a $2,000 limit.

You may also have heard of "points programs" for credit cards. Essentially, some credit cards will buy you free stuff if you use them a lot. The credit card companies do this by making business deals with certain other types of businesses – perhaps airlines, restaurant chains, or any other type of perk you want – to provide their customers with free stuff.

Why do this? Well, again, it's that sweet, sweet interest money. If the creditors can attract you to pay them interest on everything you spend, they can often negotiate better deals with other types of businesses such as airlines than you as a lone customer would not be able to negotiate for yourself.

When your credit gets really excellent, you can even get to 0% interest rates. That effectively means that you're now *not* paying interest on the money for the purchases you make, but you're still getting free stuff through rewards programs.

The same tactics – asking for a better deal because you're thinking about going to another provider – can work on other service providers as well. Internet, phone, cable, and other service providers may be willing to lower your billing plan or increase your benefits rather than losing you completely as a customer to their competitors.

These are the secrets that wealthy people know.

Lastly, I want to let my readers in on a little secret that may only work during the COVID-19 pandemic, or during a severe recession. In such frightening times it's best to have every tool in our belt. That's why it's useful to know that, during such severe circumstances, landlords and banks may be willing to put your rent payment or mortgage into forbearance.

Why? Because during times of severe national financial distress, the government often gives out cash assistance for banks and landlords whose tenants can't pay. In other words, your bank or landlord might get paid *more* by reporting that their tenants can't pay and applying for government money than they would by evicting you.

So if times are hard and you have been having trouble paying your rent or mortgage, don't be afraid to reach out to your mortgage or landlord and ask if they have a mortgage forbearance program.

#9 – Pay for Everything With a Credit Card

Now, let's be clear. This doesn't mean "spend more money than you otherwise would because you have a credit card. This means "maximize the amount of points and credit history you get by paying for everything with a credit card and putting the card on autopay to pay the full balance every month."

This technique is best for people who have credit cards with higher credit limits and more credit cards to spread the utilization between. Why? Because, as mentioned above, you want to keep your utilization to be only a small percentage of your credit limit. Spending more than 30% of your credit limit can actually *hurt* your credit score, so don't spend more than that.

But as you become a credit Zen master, you will learn the skills of juggling multiple accounts, all set to autopay, with the highest credit limits that negotiation and a good credit score can get. You will learn to choose rewards programs that give you the kinds of perks you need for fun and profit. You will learn to earn and negotiate the best interest rates.

And when you've got a low interest rate, a high credit limit, and five credit cards, all set to autopay and figured into your monthly budget, to split your monthly bills between – you can demonstrate paying off five separate credit cards every single month, and earn rewards points for free airline tickets, hotel rooms, or any other perk on every single thing you pay for.

#10 – File Your Taxes

Fun, right? You may say 'definitely not.' But it's important. This is because the federal government can *take part of your future wealth* if you don't pay your taxes.

This means that if you ever plan on becoming wealthy, you must pay your taxes. Otherwise, the late fees on your unpaid taxes will far outweigh the cost of paying your taxes on-time. This will add up to giving the government a larger cut of your future wealth than you would pay them today if you filed your taxes on time.

Once you earn more than $100,000 per year, the IRS will start paying more attention to you. If there is any suggestion that you haven't paid all the taxes you were required to pay in previous years, you may be on the hook for those taxes *plus a large amount of late fees.*

You can, however, learn a wealthy person's trick to decrease the amount of taxes deducted from your paycheck each month. By adjusting your withholdings on your W-4, you can have less money taken out of your paycheck starting with *your very next paycheck!*

Now, this may not mean you owe less taxes total. It may mean a smaller refund, or even that you owe taxes instead of getting a refund at the end of the year. But it *also* means more money in your pocket *now* to pay down debts that will otherwise charge you interest.

You can also find ways to increase your tax deductions. Tax deductions are expenses you paid doing something that the government likes and wants to promote. Because they want to encourage you to do these things – for example, attending college or owning a business, they may exempt the money you spent doing that from taxation.

Business expenses are the most common tax deductions for entrepreneurs and business owners. Everything from your home office to equipment and travel expenses may be deductible from your taxable income *if* you can prove that these expenses were necessary to allow you to run a profitable business.

For those of us who aren't business owners yet, common deductions include a variety of tax credits for college students, deductions for caring for a child or other dependent person (someone for whom you paid 50% or more of all expenses last year), tax deductions for paying medical and dental bills, and tax deductions for contributing money to licensed non-profit charities, and tax deductions for interest paid on your mortgage payments.

Note that you will need receipts to prove these expenses, so it's wise to ask for written receipts for any charitable contributions, medical and dental bills, and business expenses.

When you thoroughly review the tax deductions available to you, you may be able to find a way to actually *save* money while simultaneously getting more done by engaging in tax-deductible activities. Even though wealthy people pay most of the taxes in our country, their tax rates are typically lower than that of lower to middle class people because of all the tax deductions they get because of owning businesses, leveraging several tax laws. Tax rates on income from certain investments are also lower than tax rates on salaries and other earned income for people of most income brackets.

If you don't have your own business idea, there are several online, home-based businesses you could start to gain tax deductions right away. Our company also offers a way to start a home-based business as an affiliate and earn income while having the benefit of business tax deductions. There are thousands of opportunities out there, you just have to look.

Moral of the story: start a business, get deductions, and pay your taxes.

#11 – Take Care of Your Family

Expect the best; prepare for the worst. This is the mantra of the wise. By expecting the best, you are able to motivate yourself to reach for success, learn constantly, and constantly hone your financial game. But by planning for the worst, you can use those gains to ensure that your family is safe and protected if anything should ever go wrong.

One way to protect your family is to <u>talk to them about money</u>. Imagine how your life might have been different if your parents had taught you all of these tips, and helped you set up all the necessary accounts and paperwork, when you were still in your teenage years. How much better-off would you be today?

And it's not just children who may benefit from the knowledge we've shared here. Spouses, siblings, aunts, uncles, and parents can *all* learn to make more money, keep more money, build wealth, and enjoy more freedom and security by mastering these financial tips and tricks.

This isn't always comfortable. Some families, like some of you, might not like to think about their finances. Some people might think of finances only as a source of anxiety, not of security or power. But I'll repeat my mantra from earlier: **you can't correct what you don't confront.** If we want to change the way wealth, freedom, and security move in our communities, we must improve our financial education and then *actually implement these strategies.*

You may find it useful to make an accountability partner out of a friend or family member. If two or more people commit to implement these strategies and commit to achieving financial growth, *all* of you may feel more motivated, and will be able to encourage each other and enjoy each others' successes along the way.

Changing the present is how we change the future.

To ensure that your family's future is taken care of, <u>you will want to have a life insurance policy</u>. Life insurance might seem unnecessary today, but it may also be the best investment you ever make.

Life insurance rates depend on the age and health of the individual, as well as other factors. That means that the younger and healthier you are, the better rates you can get on life insurance. You may well be able to afford hundreds of thousands of dollars in life insurance without breaking the bank.

For example, according to LifeInsurance.com a healthy 35-year-old man can get $500,000 in life insurance coverage for only $39 per month! So if he pays that $39 per month and, God forbid, he dies before the policy expires, his wife and children will get a check for $500,000 to cover the years of earnings he wasn't able to give them.

With luck, your family won't need that money in the next several years because you will be there to provide for them. But what if something does happen to you?

Since we're hoping you *won't* die soon, you're also going to want to have health insurance for every member of your family. Why?

Because the cost of *not* having health insurance is much higher than the cost of having it.

Depending on where in the country you live, a single ER visit could cost you over $1,000 as an uninsured person. A single hospitalization may put you more than $50,000 in debt.

The wealthy people know that paying $150 per month for health insurance is a *much* better gamble than risking a $50,000 fee for an uninsured hospitalization. They also know that those with health insurance – those who are able to afford routine visits to doctors with relatively low co-pays thanks to their insurance – are less likely to become so seriously ill that they require hospitalization.

If you do not have health insurance and you have not investigated Healthcare.gov, I encourage you to do so today. President Obama's Health Insurance Marketplace offers assistance in paying health insurance premiums for *most* families and individuals. Most people who aren't already covered by Medicaid or an employers' health insurance can buy health insurance for $50-$150 per person, instead of the $400-$500 per person that may be charged by insurance companies outside of the Affordable Care Act marketplace.

These insurance premiums may end up saving you hundreds or thousands of dollars per year in overall healthcare expenses.

And that's what wealthy people do, right? They calculate their best cost-benefit arrangement.

While you're at it, you want to make sure that you have a will. Yes, like in the movies – a document that specifies who inherits which of your assets if you die.

You may assume this process is simple but settling inheritance can be complicated if you don't leave any instructions behind. Even a simple piece of paper specifying that you want to leave everything to another individual you have designated can ensure that that happens, instead of your assets getting fought over or snarled up in court.

#12 – Invest Into Your Future

Finally, it's time to start talking about investing.

Investments are *not* for people who still have uncontrolled debt, or whose two emergency funds aren't full yet. Why is that? Well, many investment plans charge heavy tax penalties if you take the money out of the account before a specified date. That means that you can't assume the money you have in investments will be available to you in the event of an emergency.

You can't afford *not* to have an emergency fund. You can't afford a $200 pair of sneakers if you don't have $2,000 in your mini emergency fund. You can't afford to be picking up the tab for friends at the bar if you don't have two months' expenses in your true emergency fund. And you can't afford to set the example to your children of behaving this way: their world may be different than ours, and they may need emergency funds in the bank even more than we do.

Instead, investing is another master-level financial technique. Putting money into investments will allow you to make much more money in the long run than simply spending money on luxuries or putting it under the mattress, but you should put money into investments *only after* your emergency funds are full and most of your debts are paid off.

What does investing really mean? Do I mean purchasing stocks and bonds which grow over time?

Well, that's one way to do it. It's certainly a fairly predictable, time-tested way. But it's not the *only* way to invest money into growing for your future. Other places to invest can include investing in property, and investing in a business or side gig that can one day produce passive income for you.

Passive income is income that you don't have to work for. It's income that you instead earn because you *own* something. You own property, or you own stake in a company. You are now entitled to part of the profits that that property or company generates.

For me, my first investment in my future was getting involved in Affiliate Marketing, or what some refer to also as Network Marketing. Though I had a full-time job when I started this "side gig," I soon learned that by properly applying the skills and knowledge being taught at affiliate marketing seminars, I could make much more money by making my "side gig" full-time than I could by keeping my day job.

The investment I made in my future by joining an affiliate marketing organization set the stage for my subsequent financial success. That's one of the reasons I started Novae in 2014: to give others the opportunity to reach financial success in the affiliate marketing industry by owning their own business with our company.

One of the most underrated investments out there, in my opinion, is personal growth and self-development. Some people even mock the idea of people paying money to be taught how to excel in their careers or personal lives. But these programs make a real difference in what a person can achieve. We'll discuss exactly how and why in our later chapter on entertainment and education.

Personal growth and self-development seminars have been the best purchases I've ever made. In fact, I don't see it as money that left my hands; I see and cherish the **investment** I made into these seminars because the results have yielded millions for me! These seminars completely transformed my life path and my beliefs about myself. These seminars made the book before you today possible.

A good mantra for personal growth is this: **get comfortable being uncomfortable**.

Change is scary. It's uncomfortable. To make financial growth happen, you may have to give up some short-term luxuries to which you've become accustomed. You may have to start doing things that you have anxiety about, or that you're not sure you can succeed in.

Don't let that stop you. All of us start out uncertain of our ability to succeed. All of us start out feeling like we're behind the pack in some way, and the kind of success discussed here just isn't for us.

You know what makes the difference between those who succeed and those who fail? Their willingness to be uncomfortable. Success stories persevere *even though* it is uncomfortable and requires change, uncertainty, and trying new things. People who don't succeed in changing their situation are often those who are too afraid to even try making major changes in their behavior.

People are so anxious to change their situation, yet unwilling to change themselves.

Another key ingredient of success is getting friends who share your values. Remember how I mentioned accountability partners earlier? Sometimes, the friends and family you already have can become your like-minded friends who are also driven to achieve financial security, power, and freedom.

But sometimes, that might *not* happen. It's hard to teach an old dog new tricks, and people who aren't as motivated as you are to create financial success may be more interested in preserving your comfortable, current habits than in pushing you and holding you accountable for taking action to make change.

That's why you'll likely need new friends. Your best assets and allies on this journey will be friends who are *already walking this walk* and focusing their thinking on excelling financially. Even if they are not already walking it, they aspire to find out how they can after they are exposed to the information. That was me, when I started my entrepreneurship journey at 20 years old.

Get around the right people and you will be amazed at the incredible strides you will be able to see in your life! These people can even mentor you.

For me, these new friends were the people I met through my affiliate marketing group. They shared my values and were more experienced with the challenges and pitfalls of just starting out on the path to financial literacy.

Now, it's worth noting: your new friends should be people who have successful habits and ambitions, even if they don't have successful results yet. It's important to understand that success takes time.

But your mentors, they should be *successful and possess the character, skills, and lifestyle that you desire to have.* Self-proclaimed mentors and coaches who sit around talking about business but who can't pay their own bills, let alone steadily grow their income and their net worth, are unlikely to be able to help you in this work. They may even hold you back by encouraging you to stay in old, unsuccessful patterns.

This is why it is critically important to remain a student until you arrive. And when you arrive, you will know because many people will give you the gift of leadership and you will be living the life of your dreams. But until this point, continue to remain humble and hungry and strive for success everyday. Because you can achieve it!

A Powerful Future

Imagine what your children will be able to achieve when you teach them all of these techniques. Imagine your children being able to optimize and move money like the most expert investors and most skilled business minds.

Financial success is only part of the picture of future justice. But as we've seen so graphically in recent electoral seasons, money often *is* power.

Let's consolidate some of that power for ourselves and *our* communities.

Chapter 4

The Entertainment and Education Connection

"What entertains us trains us."

- Reco M. McCambry

In previous chapters we've seen some of the educational problems facing the Black community in America. This problem hits us on several fronts.

It's useful to be aware of all the ways in which racism can affect our children's learning in matters of school, career, finance, and wealth. Most of these challenges are challenges we can actively counteract in our homes by educating ourselves and making education – through school or otherwise – a priority for our children in our homes.

As you read this list, I encourage you to jot down a plan for how *you* can improve every possible item on this list for your children.

Some items might sound impossible to change, like the public school funding system and systematic discrimination in hiring. But don't worry – in the next few chapters we will discuss political involvement, which is a front where you *can* actually influence those facts of life by taking a few hours each week to be involved in your city and state government's decisions.

1. A racist public school funding system which ties the quality of a child's education to the wealth of their parents.

2. Discrimination in property ownership, hiring, and finance which add up to most Black children lacking access to private schools and living in the most underfunded public school

districts in the country.

3. Learning distractions caused by poverty. Children facing hunger, violence, and financial insecurity at home often find it harder to concentrate on lessons or view schoolwork as the highest priority in their lives.

4. Lack of parental support at home. Black parents who may have faced the same challenges to their own education may not be able to help their children prioritize learning and complete challenging homework assignments if they did not learn the material themselves, or are required to work more than one job to keep food on the table.

5. Lack of representation and positive role models of their own race and gender. When students don't see many highly educated, academically successful role models who look like them in the media or in the neighborhood, they can internalize the belief that people like them can't succeed in school or in legal high-paying jobs.

6. Lack of finance and business education in public schools – this education is often provided only by wealthy families to their children at home.

7. Lack of political education in schools. We'll discuss what "political education" is and the enormous difference it can make to our communities in a future chapter.

All of this, of course, can add up to a vicious cycle. When we face challenges with our education – especially challenges that lead to generational financial insecurity – it's that much more difficult to help our children succeed in school. Whether we're forced to work outside the home 80 hours per week to put food on the table or we struggle with math and reading ourselves, it can be difficult for us to help our children succeed when we had difficulty succeeding ourselves.

The good news is, school is not the only place to get an education. Childhood is not the only time for education. As I mentioned earlier, I actually got my most valuable education outside of school, through business, financial education, and personal development seminars. It was this adult education, which I obtained for myself outside of college or any other degree program, which has made the biggest difference in my family's financial future.

There are many Black millionaires and scholars who did not even learn to read until they were in their teens or later. Prioritizing elementary school education gives our kids every advantage. But history has shown many times over that enterprising Black people can attain a high degree of learning which permits runaway financial success, and even academic and artistic excellence, at any point in life.

Now, reading this, you might be thinking "that doesn't sound very Black." It is a tragic fact that in some places, "Black culture" is considered to be a culture that looks down on formal education. I have even seen Black children and teens get bullied by their classmates and peers for bringing home excellent grades and test scores. The idea that it's not "cool" to do well in school still pervades some local cultures.

In a way, it is easy to understand how this happens. So-called "laziness" is often a reaction to forced labor. When people of any age are forced to do a certain type of work and aren't given access to the rewards of that labor, the natural response is to stop working. Under those circumstances, people who *do* work for the system can actually be seen as a threat to the rebellion.

But we don't live in the 19th century anymore. We live in an era where, if we play our cards right, we *can* keep the fruits of our labor. We can build up tremendous wealth, power, and freedom using the same hands and minds that were exploited by whites to build their own wealth for centuries. We will face challenges, but these are not insurmountable. Especially if we have the support of a strong community.

The good news is, even in places where success in school is sometimes frowned upon, Black culture has a *strong* tradition of working hard. We just tend to do it in the ways that we see as having the highest potential benefit for us.

Everybody knows a hustler. A hustler is an aggressively enterprising person, also known as a "go-getter." But in Black culture, this label can have both positive and negative connotations.

The positive hustler is someone who is always selling a product, service, or idea that benefits their community and achieves economic gain. The negative hustler is someone who sells products that *harm* their community, or takes part in illegal activities and organized crime for economic gain.

Both seek economic progress expeditiously. Often, both feel that they are doing the right thing by securing economic gain for themselves and their families. But unfortunately, the latter also causes harm to themselves and those around them.

Negative hustlers are also what most people picture when they picture a Black "hustler," because the positive hustlers who create great wealth by doing something that *benefits* their communities do not get equal media attention.

And everybody knows that hustlers are some of the smartest, most innovative, strategic, and hard-working people in America. I once knew a business school professor who was acquainted with some drug dealers. "If those boys applied the same kind of strategy and tactics on Wall Street," he said to me, "they'd be dominating the U.S. stock market."

The tragedy, of course, is that the negative hustlers often engage in behavior that's destructive toward both themselves and their communities. Most know they are unlikely to stay alive and out of jail past the age of forty, and if they are selling drugs they know that their products destroy the lives of people in their communities. Many even engage in the murder of their own community members to protect their personal or immediate family's cashflow and freedom. Many simply see this as the *only* way for them to experience success or provide for their families.

It's easy to understand how these behaviors came about. And by understanding this, we can change them. We can shift all of that amazing energy, ingenuity, and dedication into the kinds of legal career paths and financial strategy that can allow these same kids who are ending up in prisons today to dominate the U.S. economy tomorrow.

For a good chunk of American history, illegal professions were the most lucrative and ethical jobs open to Black people. This started early in American history, when Black people were not allowed to own property at all, and when freeing people from slavery was itself an illegal activity.

This time period included the eras of Black codes and Jim Crow when we could expect financial success to be violently punished. Some of our ancestors probably decided "well, we might as well live fast and die young, because that's the only way we can expect to achieve wealth and power for any period of time."

The good news is, we don't live in that era anymore. We still face challenges to obtaining wealth and power that white people *don't*, but we now live in a cultural and legal system where we can be *more* sure of wealth, power, and freedom through academic success and legal jobs. That may indeed be why the illegal path to wealth is still so glorified: perhaps the powers that be don't *want* us to realize that these venues to generational wealth and freedom are now legally open to us and quite achievable.

If we play our cards right – and goodness knows, hustlers are masters of strategy and execution – we can gain the kind of wealth that brings *lasting* power, not just temporary power, to our families and communities.

The bad news is, to our children today, it can still often *feel* like we are living in that era. When Black children struggle for basic food, shelter, and security at home, it's easy for them to resent school and feel that it is an unfair and unimportant imposition on their time.

When they look at their neighborhoods and see that most of the Black adults they know dropped out of school, or are not paid fairly for their labor, it's easy to feel that school and traditional career paths are not good or realistic investments for them.

When they look at popular Black media and see that it's gang members and drug dealers who are being glorified as models of Black success – not doctors, lawyers, scientists, or businessmen – it's easy to feel that school is actually a burdensome *distraction* from the most realistic and desirable paths to success for Black youth.

Changing all of that won't be easy. It starts at home. It starts with educating *ourselves* as Black adults so that we set an example of highly educated and informed adulthood for Black youth. It starts with teaching our children – and *showing* them through exposure to Black role models – the statistical fact that their best shot at lasting success, power, and fame is through excelling in school and legal career paths.

Over time, these actions that each of us take at home each day will add up to create neighborhoods and a popular culture which supports the *real* most effective paths to success for Black youth – not the ones that lead to short lifespans and mass incarceration.

There might be another obvious thought in your mind as you are reading this. "But Reco," you might be thinking, "so much of what is considered 'Black culture' nationally is dedicated to glorifying rappers, athletes, and overly sexualized female role models.

Yes. And that's where the "entertainment" in this chapter title comes in.

We usually think of education and entertainment as two separate things. In fact, they are not. *Every single thing* that goes into our brain is education. Everything we see, hear, or become aware of teaches us something about the world.

My own success came from what I watched, read, and listened to. In my case, I chose to listen to audio and watch videos about entrepreneurship, financial education, business success, personal growth and self-development instead of just listening to rap music. Growing up, I did listen to Tupac, the Notorious B.I.G., Master P, Too Short, and Snoop Dog. Even in my college days I listened to TI, Outkast, Ludacris, Cash Money Millionaires, and others.

I could relate to many of the lyrics in these songs because of the environment I grew up in. But I realized that even though I grew up in that environment, I didn't want to *end* up there.

After I realized that rapping and athletics were not going to get me to the life I wanted to live, I began to search for other answers. That's when I found out about entrepreneurship and the "real secret" to wealth – what's in your head.

When I realized how much these listening and reading materials could help me succeed financially, build wealth for my family, and become truly successful, it was an obvious choice.

Glorifying drug dealing, gang violence, and sexualizing women was going to get me absolutely nowhere in life. Listening to financial education, going to seminars, and watching and listening to personal development audios and videos, on the other hand, helped me see new ways to accumulate more wealth, power, and confidence. Once I realized that, it was a no-brainer.

It might sound painful to give up the education you've become accustomed to. It might sound unpleasant to talk to your kids and teenagers about changing the media they consume. It's easy to understand why gangsta rap and other glorifications of Black-on-Black violence might be hard to give up. So often American popular culture offers so few representations of people who look like us, much less people who look like us possessing power and enjoying themselves.

But it's a trap. And it should be a clue that they call some of the most popular music of today "Trap Music."

We all know the statistics. The life of the high-rolling drug dealer is a temporary fantasy that leads to an ultimate demise. In the real world, almost all gangstas end up shot dead or behind bars at an early age, leaving their children without wealth or power, and with huge holes in their hearts where their parents used to be.

It is my belief, that the oppressors, the same lineage of oppressors that sought to hang us from trees and beat us to death, are the same oppressors who allow certain music to be produced for millions of our people to hear. If they couldn't continue to outright do violence to us, then why not find ways to make us demonize and kill ourselves? That is exactly what we see in music today. Believe it or not, this music isn't meant to entertain our community; instead it is meant to teach and train our community, controlling our actions and ambitions. This should be a wake-up call to us all.

We've got to put a stop to that. And here's how we do it.

Glorifying the "True Gangsta"

So many of the facets of Black culture that hold us and our children back today formed in direct response to oppression. A dislike of school comes from the fact that, for most of American history, we weren't allowed to keep most of the benefits of a great education for ourselves. The glorification of illegal professions and violence comes from the fact that, for a long time, these seemed like the most feasible paths to success for Black people in a discriminatory society.

So how do we reverse these destructive cultural realities? By telling ourselves and our kids what's in it for *us*.

We can keep the work of our hands and minds now. A cold, hard look at the balance sheet shows that we create *more* wealth and power for ourselves and our communities by breaking from the glorified cultures like gangsta rap and trap music and taking power in the legal – and currently white-dominated – halls of power such as Wall Street, Washington, and the Ivory Tower.

We can change our motivations by realizing that gangsta rap or trap music is not a roadmap to real, lasting, generational success. *It is a distraction from it.*

Black people are used to being played. We're used to being on the lookout for who's trying to fool us or undermine us. Well, this is one of those cases. Gangsta culture – everything that tells us we must harm fellow Black people, or risk death or incarceration to be successful – is a diversionary tactic.

I propose a *new* definition of gangsta. In today's language, let's define a "gangsta" as someone who is powerful, glamorous, intelligent, and wealthy. Someone who defied all the odds stacked up against them to accomplish levels of success that were thought once impossible. By this definition, individuals like President Barack Obama and Oprah Winfrey are two of the most gangsta Black people of the 21st century.

Unfortunately, "gangsta" today still usually refers to someone who does violence against members of their own community and who has a high risk of being murdered or incarcerated before the age of 40.

Let's shift the positive aspects of the "gangsta" stereotype into paths that are even more clever than those of the drug dealer. Even more dedicated to their community than the gang member.

Let's make "gangsta" a term that refers to any successful Black person – especially those who support their *whole* Black community – not just part of it. Let's apply "gangsta" those who build generational wealth and political change, not just fleeting bling. The "gangstas" of tomorrow are those who do this with great and fearless intention. It takes courage to succeed the right way. By not quitting. By looking your opposition in the face, and persevering anyway. Now that's gangsta!

Practices that discriminate against Black status symbols like expensive jewelry, fly shoes/clothing, and certain hairstyles are just that – discriminatory. There's no reason we can't preserve a great deal of our culture that is uniquely Black, and bring it to Wall Street with us.

But we all know that there *are* parts of today's Black culture which are harmful to our children. Glorifying violence, illegal activities, and a "live fast, die young" mindset only ensures that our children will *not* build the generational wealth and real political change that will give our people true wealth and power.

And maybe that's part of why these art forms have been allowed to become so successful by a society that continues to discriminate and profit off of the forced labor of impoverished and incarcerated Black people.

It is worth noting that the "state of hip-hop culture" isn't totally lost. Many rap artists and entertainers share the views in this book, and are becoming a loud voice for social justice and progress in the Black community. Rap artists such as Jay Z, J. Cole, Kendrick Lamar, Killer Mike, and TI are a few examples of the many rappers who are starting to make social justice and progress part of their life's mission in their music. They are also showing support to organizations that champion this cause.

Charlamagne Tha God and the hip-hop radio show "The Breakfast Club" has become a massively important platform to spread awareness and educate the Black community on our history and possibilities for our future. This show has featured some of the most progressive Black thought leaders of our time.

It is time for all Black musical artists and entertainers to use their influence to consciously shape the minds of the millions of fans they inspire across the world. It is time to become the change we want to see in the world, if we want to expedite and guarantee the success of our future generations.

Even though many hip-hop historians have expressed their dislike in today's modern version of rap music and the artists that produce lyrics that don't elevate our culture, I am optimistic that some of the hip-hop artists of this generation will step up and champion this cause of social justice and progress. For example, I was pleased to hear lyrics of the song recently released "The Bigger Picture" by rapper Lil Baby. The lyrics place listeners in the shoes of this 25-year-old and show the injustice he faces in Black America from his perspective.

The song, which was released just a couple of weeks after the senseless killing of George Floyd, racked up more than 65 million audio and video streams from its release through June 25th, according to Nielsen Music/MRC Data. The music video, in addition to his reach with over 14 million fans between Instagram and Twitter, positions him to influence those that follow his lead in this venture of social justice and progress.

In addition to Lil Baby, other highly successful artists including Meek Mill, Beyoncé, H.E.R., and Trey Songz have released songs to their millions of fans and followers on social media which are inspiring change and getting everyone more behind this mission for change. Even new talent is being unveiled as Keedron Bryant's "I Just Wanna Live" went viral and landed the 12-year-old a record deal with Warner Records. Many of our entertainers are utilizing their platforms to forge change by bringing more awareness to these issues and their support of the movement.

If we band together and take a stand against entertainment that is produced to further separate, demonize, and kill our communities; then we will begin to unify, liberate, and give birth to the world that our ancestors dreamed of many years ago. Success in all areas will be a reality!

Steps You Can Take Today

One of the first rules you learn in business is the way to get things done. How do you do that? You come up with concrete, measurable goals, and then come up with concrete, measurable steps to take over time to meet those goals.

I'm going to pose an ambitious challenge to you. I'm going to challenge you to rise to the occasion and create transformative change for yourself and your family.

How are we going to do that? We're going to substitute *all of your gangsta media consumption* with financial education, business education and self-development consumption.

Don't worry. We won't do this overnight. Because that's the other secret that all great businessmen know: you have to do things in small steps in order to create lasting change. Trying to change everything overnight just won't work.

So here is your new road map for success:

Week 1

For up to *one hour per day*, replace your streaming music service, Grand Theft Auto, or any other entertainment that glorifies violence and the exploitation and objectification of Black people (including Black women!) with financial education, professional education, self-help, or personal development audios or YouTube video. I've got a collection of YouTube videos or inspirational audios that are available to you if you're not sure where to start.

These media can be whatever you feel you need most. If your first priority is to get wealthy without having to change your job duties, you might prioritize financial education. If you know there's a skill or certification that you can get a pay raise by earning, you might choose to study that. If you know there's an area causing distress in your life, maybe look for self-help podcasts or support groups about that.

If you just want to know how the most successful people get it done, you might look for personal development media from top performers. You can find all of this through my company Novae in our Inspirational Media. We offer live seminars around the country, FREE weekly webinars and FREE weekly mentorship conference calls.

If you're spending less than an hour per day consuming media or surfing the Internet as it is, you don't have to add entertainment time to meet this goal. But consume your one hour per day of education in how *you* can achieve *real* success before you move on to escapist entertainment.

To make sure that you *actually do this*, I encourage you to write or print out a physical checklist. Physically check off your one hour of "success education" when you complete it each day.

There aren't a lot of things that are more satisfying than setting a goal and completing it each day. But I'll bet you'll find something that *is* even more rewarding than checking off those boxes on your list. I'll bet you'll start to notice real quick that you are getting much more satisfaction and benefit from your new choice of entertainment than from your old choices.

Week 2

Now, I challenge you to add an additional hour to your daily task list. Chances are, after a week of listening to transformative audios and videos, you have learned a lot of things you can do for your own success.

When you're making your new checklist for the week, I'd like you to add a new box. One hour daily of consuming success entertainment, and one hour per day of *actually performing the activities described in these audios and videos*.

That might mean getting on the phone to your creditors to fix your credit score and get better benefits. It might mean actually brainstorming, budgeting, and strategizing for your personal financial optimization or your business sales optimization. It might mean meditating or doing physical exercises, or doing research to find a psychotherapist in your area that you can afford. It might mean going to AA meetings.

Whatever it is, just make sure you're spending an hour a day *doing something to improve your life.*

Just like last week, I absolutely promise that you'll be stunned by your gains. You'll be stunned by how differently you think, feel, and act. You'll be stunned by how many benefits you are getting, whether these be financial or emotional. Just one hour a day of going above and beyond what you do in your normal daily life is all it takes.

Week 3

Can you guess what I'm going to say? That's right. Add another hour. If you don't have three hours per day to consume entertainment, that's quite understandable. Working, going to school, and spending facetime with our family or community are three of the most important things we can do for our long-term success already.

But if there are some days where you spend hours and hours watching TV, surfing the Internet, or listening to rap music, I challenge you to complete *three hours* of success education or action each day *before* you start in on your old forms of media.

Check off those boxes on that list.

By now you might find that once you get started working toward real success for yourself and your family, you don't want to stop.

Week 4

Can you guess what I'm gonna say? You're right. This fourth and final week of your progression, I'm going to pose you the ultimate challenge. If you can meet it, you'll be amazed by how your life changes.

Starting this week – and never, ever stopping – I'd like you to spend *four hours* on success education and action each day before you start into your old forms of entertainment.

This might still leave you with time to indulge in your own past times on the weekends. But it will also put you on the ultra-fast-track to success, whatever that looks like for you.

Remember to strategize based on your own life situation and current level of education. "Success education" might look different for you depending on what your current skill level is and what industry you work in.

If you never learned about interest rates, negotiating with creditors, and other secrets to financial success as a kid, you might prioritize basic financial education and strategy.

If you're interested in entrepreneurship and building wealth by becoming your own boss, it might mean consuming media from affiliate or multilevel marketing (MLM) conference calls and meetings. MLM education is extremely useful for all entrepreneurs and businesspeople, even if you don't join or buy products from the organization. After all, the function of these trainings is to make you a better overall businessperson so that the MLM network will benefit from your skills.

If you already work in a career path where you know you can easily get a pay raise by learning new skills, completing new certifications, or applying to more lucrative jobs, you might spend your time learning those skills, earning those certifications, or learning from career coaches and recruiters how to optimize your cover letters, resumes, and interviews before firing your applications off.

You might prioritize finding ways to save money so you can use it to build wealth through budgeting and frugal living. You might prioritize learning the best way to support your kids both academically and socially through their school careers. You might prioritize learning how to get involved in your city and state lawmaking processes, and then actually showing up to help change the laws you live under. Which sounds like the best fit for your personality and interests?

Whatever it is, it's going to get you and your children and community further than you ever dreamed possible. Even if you don't know where to start, start somewhere. Hopefully these steps will prove beneficial as you get started on your journey.

Chapter 5

Fierce Leadership:
The Essential Skills Needed

"The greatest tragedy in life is not death, but a life without a purpose."
-Dr. Myles Munroe

One of the greatest leadership teachers of our time is Dr. Myles Munroe. As I watched one of his seminars on Youtube, Dr. Munroe, opened his lecture about how to become a great leader in a wonderful way: he tells us who these skills are intended for.

"This is for housewives, students, mechanics, clerks. This session is for nursery workers, politicians, and kings. This session is for secretaries. It's for masons and carpenters."

How many of us think of ourselves as leaders? How many of us think, "Oh, talk of leadership is for someone else. It's for someone younger or older than me. It's for someone of a different career or income level. It's for some one of a different gender or skill set."

No. Leadership is for all of us. Only when we *all* develop the leadership potential for ourselves can our communities collectively lead our cities, states, and countries. Only then can we achieve an equal and free future.

We can lead in different ways, to be sure. We need political and social justice leaders to change laws and public opinion. We need financial and business leaders to build wealth and resources. We need academic and creative leaders to seek truth and create culture. We need religious leaders to build community and spiritual power. We need leaders in the home to raise our kids to be better leaders than we will ever be by giving them advantages, education, and inspiration that we never had growing up.

Leadership is not a job title. It sure isn't something other people give you. I'm sure any of us can think of a boss, politician, or other "leader" who is hilariously ineffectual and even harmful toward those around them. We may ask ourselves how those people got into power.

Maybe they got there in a bad way. Maybe they have learned to gain power for themselves at the success of others. Maybe they abandon their communities in order to achieve personal success. Maybe they manipulate others with pretty words that aren't matched by beneficial actions.

Well here's the truth: it doesn't matter. It doesn't matter who's in power if they're not doing what a leader is supposed to do. If they're not improving the success of everyone around them, if they're not creating better well-being, power, knowledge, and spirit for their family, company, community, or church, they're not a real leader.

Why is that difference important? For the same reason that real success is different from gangsta success. False leadership – leaders who harm others – their power is temporary. They can only hang onto it for so long. And when they fall from grace, others are likely to turn against them just as they once preyed on others.

Real leadership creates real power. Real leadership creates power from *community*. A real leader empowers others along with themselves. This might sound like a selfless act, but it's not a sacrifice. When a real leader falls upon hard times, there are a thousand other leaders who *they empowered* waiting to lift them back up as they once lifted others.

That's the self-serving angle. The large angle should be obvious. When we focus on empowering others within our community, we *build community power*. Community power always gets more done than individual power.

One leader can only do so much. A thousand leaders can do anything. If each of *them* trains a thousand more leaders, they have trained a nation that can lead the world.

So where does *true* leadership come from? How do you accomplish it?

There are a few traits that distinguish leaders who succeed in building real power for their communities. We'll discuss these – and steps you can take to obtain each of them – in the pages to come.

But first, we've already seen the power of learning by example. When we *see* how a thing is possible, and what it looks like, that's much more powerful than any how-to manual we could ever find.

So who are some examples of great Black leaders of the past? And what made them so successful?

Harriet Tubman

Harriet Tubman was an incredible leader who risked her life many times in the service of others. She served in every way imaginable, from preaching and writing to building wealth, fighting in the Civil War, building new community resources for Black people, and later engaging in the fight to allow women like herself to vote in U.S. elections.

Even before the outbreak of the Civil War, Harriet Tubman was called "Moses" by many people thanks to her groundbreaking work in leading Black people out of slavery. She escaped slavery herself – and then risked her life by returning to slaveholding territory *thirteen times* to help other enslaved people to find freedom in the northern states and Canada as she had done.

Tubman was an important "conductor" for the network of abolitionist safehouses known as the Underground Railroad. By carefully working with a network of contacts who wanted to help freed slaves, she guided more than 70 enslaved people into free territory. Tubman is said to have "never lost a passenger" – that is, none of the people she was helping were ever caught or killed. She did this all with the knowledge that she was viewed as a threat by slaveholding authorities, and would likely be shot on sight if she were spotted.

Harriet was referred to as "General Tubman" by John Brown, a white abolitionist who sought to build an "army" to fight slavery years before the outbreak of the Civil War. She recruited many formerly enslaved people to his cause, and helped him to develop detailed logistical plans for his 1859 raid on Harpers Ferry.

Brown's raid failed to achieve its goal of assisting slaves in staging an armed revolt against plantation owners and Brown was ultimately executed for his attempt. But the example set by the "army" who was prepared to fight for the freedom of slaves forced many abolitionists to confront the evils of their own tolerance for slavery, and has been called a "dressed rehearsal" for the Civil War by some scholars.

Tubman later became the first woman to lead an armed operation for the Union Army. She initially served as a scout and a spy thanks to her bravery and intimate knowledge of slaveholding territory. In 1863, she led the 54th Massachusetts Infantry Regiment – a regiment consisting entirely of Black Union soldiers – in a raid which freed over 750 Black people from slavery in one day. Many of the liberated people went on to join the Union army and fight for the freedom of all enslaved people in the Confederacy.

Harriet Tubman was even able to enjoy domestic bliss and a secure retirement after the war – due largely to her own wealth- and community-building efforts. After purchasing a farm in New York State, she moved her parents there and cared for them until they passed away. During this time she was active in the cause of women's suffrage, believing the world would be a better place if women, including herself, were allowed to vote for laws and politicians.

She herself eventually entered the care of a retirement home for Black people that she herself had helped establish a few years earlier. In this way, Tubman's ceaseless service and community-building paid off. By organizing Black people and creating community resources that hadn't even existed before her birth, she created the community that she and her children needed to live a secure life after the Civil War.

Madame C.J. Walker

Born Sarah Breedlove, Madam C. J. Walker was the first American woman to become a self-made millionaire. This is all the more remarkable considering her early life.

Walker was born in Louisiana just two years after the end of the Civil War. If that weren't intimidating enough, she was also orphaned by the age of seven after her mother died in a cholera epidemic. She learned to read through Sunday school lessons at her church, and began working as a domestic servant at the age of 10. She eventually began working as a laundress, which paid better, but still less than a dollar a day.

After marrying and having a daughter of her own, Madam Walker became determined to provide more for her children. At the same time, she was afflicted by severe hair and skin care problems arising from her work with harsh chemicals in her job. Fortunately, her brothers were barbers who knew a thing or two about the health of Black hair and skin. Walker first worked selling hair and skin products produced by another Black woman entrepreneur, Annie Malone, before deciding she could improve on the recipes and the business model.

Walker eventually surpassed Annie Malone's success through her Madam C. J. Walker Manufacturing Company. As she gained wealth through shrewd business dealings and tireless work ethic, Madam Walker began to use her wealth to help other American Black people who faced rampant discrimination in the years after the Civil War.

She joined the National Negro Business League and provided funds for the creation of institutions for Black people including the

Tuskeegee Institute, the Bethel African Methodist Episcopal Church, and Mary McLeod Bethune's Daytona Education and Industrial School for Negro Girls (which later became Bethune-Cookman University).

During World War I she was a leader in the Circle for Negro War Relief which benefitted Black World War I veterans. Around the same time she joined the National Association for the Advancement of Colored People and became one of the organization's largest donors. She was honored for her large donation to the preservation of Frederick Douglass' Anacostia House by the National Association of Colored Women's Clubs.

Malcolm X

Born Malcolm Little, Malcolm X was a Black leader who preached about Black power, racial justice, social justice, and economic justice during the mid-20th century. Though some of his views are controversial, such as the idea that Black society must be separate from white society in order to be truly free, he is remembered as a pioneer of Black community organizing and political activism.

Many cite him and Dr. Martin Luther King, Jr. as two teachers who pair well together. While King focused on nonviolence and the right of Black Americans to participate equally in an integrated society, Malcolm X focused on the need for Black Americans to be prepared to defend and rely on themselves, and to cultivate power, mutual support, and a sense of identity within their own communities.

Like MLK, Macolm X was a minister's son. He was an admirer of Marcus Garvey, whose message about the power of an autonomous, unified Black community resonated strongly with young Malcolm. Malcolm X's father was a leader of Garvey's Universal Negro Improvement Association and African Communities League, and his mother was a reporter for Garvey's newspaper, *Negro World*. These strong examples of leadership and activism doubtless encouraged Malcolm X to take a leadership role in improving his community later in life.

Young Malcolm's family moved from Nebraska to Minnesota and then Michigan, fleeing threats of violence from the Ku Klux Klan who became enraged by the family's activities. When young Malcolm's father died in a streetcar accident, the rumors that he had in fact been murdered by racists must have made an indelible impression in Malcolm X's mind. His mother became hospitalized from a nervous breakdown a few years later, so Malcolm spent his teenage years living in a series of foster homes.

Malcolm X aspired to be a lawyer, but dropped out of school after a white high school teacher told him that was not a realistic goal for a Black man (the teacher used the N-word instead of 'Black man'). Malcolm recalled feeling that indeed the white world offered few opportunities for him as a Black man, and that there wasn't much point to continuing his formal education for that reason. Like so many Black youth of today, Malcolm X made money through illegal activities including selling drugs, gambling, pimping, and robbery during his late teenage years and early adult life.

While in prison for a robbery, young Malcolm met a self-educated Black fellow inmate who inspired in him a love for reading, and a belief that Black men could command respect through knowledge. At the same time, his siblings wrote to him about the Nation of Islam – a religious movement preaching about the necessity for Black people to become self-reliant and eventually return to Africa. After beginning to practice the teachings of Islam in his life, Malcolm felt that the Nation's teachings were the missing key to obtaining self-respect as a Black man.

At this time he adopted the name "Malcolm X" for the first time. All Nation of Islam members were encouraged to begin using "X" as their last name, as a stand-in for their *true* ancestral African family names which were lost and could not be known because of the slave trade.

Malcolm X went on to become regarded as the second-most influential leader of the Nation of Islam. Though he eventually left the Nation over disagreements with its other leadership, Malcolm X supported the Nation of Islam's social welfare programs such as its free drug rehabilitation program.

Tragically, Malcolm X was assassinated just a few years before MLK. Malcolm X had received death threats from Nation of Islam members due to his public criticism of the organization's leadership, but was also under FBI surveillance at the time of his death just like Martin Luther King, Jr.. To this day, debate rages in some circles over whether Malcolm X was assassinated by a member of the very Black power organization he had once supported, or by the government in an attempt to suppress Black power everywhere, or a combination of the two!

Today Malcolm X is remembered as a complicated figure who held some beliefs that are problematic to some, but who was still highly successful in organizing Black Americans to work for their own self-betterment and that of their communities. Many educational centers and streets are named in his honor.

Dr. Martin Luther King, Jr.

Everybody and their grandmother has probably talked to you about Dr. Martin Luther King, Jr.. He's just about the only Black leader from history that people routinely talk about. But there are a lot of things you probably don't know about Dr. King. He didn't just wake up one day ready to lead the Civil Rights Movement. He had to do a lot of boring, everyday stuff to lift up his people.

Martin Luther King, Jr. was born in 1929 in Atlanta, Georgia. As almost everybody knows, he grew up as a preacher's son and studied to follow in his father's footsteps and enter the life of a minister.

Pretty ordinary story so far, right? So what happened to make MLK *the* face of the Civil Rights movement?

Some of it probably started with a leader in his own life: Rev. Martin Luther King, Sr. Though less well-known than his son, Rev. King, Sr. was able to travel the world with the help of a supportive church community. His experience seeing the cultures and political activities of different nations, including the rise of Nazism in Germany, doubtlessly influenced the way he later taught his son about religion, social justice, and the need for a mutually supportive Black community.

His experiences also doubtlessly led Martin Luther King, Sr. to organize his own community to fight for a better world. Martin Luther King, Jr. grew up watching his father openly combat discrimination and segregation in both his personal and public lives. From refusing to accept rude or racist treatment from white police officers and store owners to leading hundreds of people to protest outside of Atlanta's City Hall, Martin Luther King, Sr. set the example of community organizing for his son. Without the father's work, it is doubtful that Martin Luther King, Jr. would have done what he did.

MLK's Civil Rights work started with bus boycotts. Today the groundbreaking refusal of Black girls and women (a 15-year-old Black girl was actually punished for refusing to give up her seat to a white man before Rosa Parks) is historically often thought of as the start of the Civil Rights movement, but imagine how *boring* it must have seemed at the time. Boycott the city buses for being segregated?

Many people of today might feel that such a cause was too boring, too inconvenient, too small, or too tedious to be worthwhile. Yet the large-scale boycott sparked by one Black woman and then turned into mass organization by one Baptist minister Martin Luther King, Jr. became the start of sweeping changes to racist legislation all across America.

King went on to consistently advocate for anti-racist actions including boycotts, protests, and civil disobedience across America. He used his platform as a pastor to advocate for racial justice within the Southern Christian Leadership Conference, where dozens of other

Christian and Civil Rights Leaders came to know King as a go-to servant who would help the cause of social justice in any way he could. By working reliably to serve others, he became one of the most renowned and respected leaders in the country.

King's cooperation with other Black organizers and Christian leaders eventually became so much of a threat to the racist status quo that King was assassinated in 1968. The assassin doubtlessly hoped that King's death would put a stop to his work. Instead, his murder inflamed a passion that caused millions of people across the United States to work even more fervently for racial justice, and ultimately force the passage of large numbers of laws designed to end segregation and discrimination.

This work is still not entirely done. As we've seen, both social culture and legal policies remain in place to this day which too often place Black children and workers at a disadvantage. But we have more freedom than King was born into, and we can use that freedom to create even greater change.

If, that is, we're willing to consistently show up where we are needed. Even if it's to something boring, like a bus boycott or a protest outside of City Hall.

Six Frontiers of Leadership

Leadership can seem intimidating to many of us. We may look at certain people and feel that they are just "natural leaders," and that we aren't "cut out" to lead.

This is false. Leadership is a learned set of skills, like any other skill or profession. And it is one that we often undervalue. Leadership, after all, means the potential to create change. That is something that all of us need to take into our own hands at times like the present.

So what are the *most essential* skills of leadership that aren't taught in schools? The most essential skills you must learn to become a leader are:

#1 – Managing Internal Conflicts

Many of us do not even recognize the internal conflicts that happen within ourselves. We often view our thoughts and feelings as being accurate reflections of the way things are. In fact, this is not true! Our thoughts and feelings can be affected by many things, including what we heard growing up, what we see on TV, and what people say to us in our daily lives.

This is why some people act like "natural leaders" while others view leadership as something that is beyond them. There is no real difference in the potential of these individuals: they have simply been told different things about themselves, which have created internal conflicts in their thoughts and feelings.

Some common irrational belief patterns that you will need to master within yourself in order to become a leader include:

1. **I am undeserving.** The thought or feeling that "I don't feel I deserve success," or "I can't see myself becoming a leader" will stop us in our tracks. It is also irrational and inaccurate. Learn to recognize this thought and feeling – and refuse to tolerate it!

2. **I am ordinary.** "I cannot do extraordinary things." Or, "I do not *want* to stand apart, receive attention, or be seen as different. I want to fit in." This is another thought that will prevent our efforts to make change from succeeding.

3. **I am afraid of social change.** The fear of rejection, loneliness, or criticism can also stop us in our tracks. If we

change, the people who are around us right now may not like that. But that's a necessary part of changing the world for the better. Many people are uncomfortable with change when it first begins to happen. Yet change is needed to make the world a better place.

4. **My success is short-lived.** Even when you begin to experience success, you may fear that it is temporary and you won't be able to sustain it. Don't let this thought stop you from moving forward!

5. **Perfectionism.** We can delay taking action infinitely if we feel that now is not the perfect time to take it. If we wait for ourselves, or our circumstances to be perfect – that day will never come. Come as you are, and be a leader.

6. **I can't handle the responsibility.** "I will be drained dry by others wanting things from me. I cannot get anything done because it is impossible to please everyone." So don't please everyone, then! Just do what you know is right. And you know that doing nothing is *not* the right thing to do.

#2 – External Conflicts

Internal conflicts come from ideas we learned about ourselves in the past. Often we adopt these thoughts and feelings in order to avoid external conflicts. As children and young people, we don't want to be criticized by those around us. We want to be accepted. Unfortunately, change for the better is not usually a comfortable process. Our desire to remain comfortable holds us back.

Once we begin to master our internal conflicts and become leaders, our behavior changes. This can be uncomfortable for some people around us. We begin to face external conflicts such as criticism and feelings of resentment from people around us.

It can be our parent who doubts what we are doing because they grew up in a different time. It can be our friends who resent that we no longer want to party all the time because we are making social change. It can be our organizations who don't like us "rocking the boat" by pointing out problems and advocating for better solutions.

That doesn't mean we're wrong. It means we are fighting the good fight.

A great example of this is the progress of wearing masks in the recent pandemic. At first, people who wore masks might have been considered "paranoid" or "overreacting." Many got funny looks, or even encountered anger and hostility, from other people. The reason was simple: the people didn't want to be reminded of the pandemic. They didn't want to be reminded that they were facing danger. They wanted to remain comfortable. But in this situation, like in every other, the desire to remain comfortable held them back. It actually increased their risk, and the risk faced by others around them.

As leaders, we must master our response to these external conflicts. We must do what we know to be right, regardless of how those around us react. Otherwise, we will always be imprisoned by fear.

We must learn to be the voice of reason, even in chaos. This is only possible if we learn to navigate by our internal compass, and not by the words or ideas of those around us.

Our emotional detachment from external conflicts is in fact a sign of *faith*. We can only master external conflicts through faith that we are doing the right thing, and that this thing needs to be done.

As leaders, we must make our desire to succeed in making change greater than our need to be accepted by others. Only in this way can true social change occur for our communities.

#3 – Degrees of Leadership

Leadership trainers often speak of "degrees" or "levels" of leadership. These relate to a person's mastery of internal and external conflicts. A high-level leader is one who is able to stand firm and steer the ship rightly in the midst of chaos, criticism, and disagreement. A high-level leader is also secure enough in their leadership, and good enough at *teaching* leadership, that they can elevate other people to become leaders and delegate work to them so that more can get done.

It isn't necessary for all of us to become The Leader. In fact, it's downright counterproductive! Movements are strongest when they have *as many* leaders as possible. The worst thing for a movement, be it a corporation or a social justice organization, is for leaders to start competing to be "The Leader," which often entails trying to take other leaders down and damage their work! Always remember, you can be "a" leader and not be "the" leader.

To level up in leadership, you must be focused within. Just like in our previous two steps, you can't be distracted or delayed by what other people are doing. Instead, you must focus on taking responsibility within *yourself* for making things happen. Laying blame on other people, or getting preoccupied with what they're doing, are not leadership traits. They are just the opposite.

Here are a few traits that distinguish a true high-level leader from a non-leader:

1. A non-leader is threatened by disagreement. They may see disagreement as an attack, or having an evil agenda. A high-level leader *values* disagreement. They ask themselves "what is this person seeing in the situation that I am not?"

This doesn't mean they change because someone told them to. It means they investigate concerns and disagreements to see where the grain of truth lies, and how it can make their cause stronger. In the process of listening to and valuing those who disagree, they help to bring them onboard with the plan and grow the plan's support base!

2. A non-leader feels the need to prove themselves, even if it means doing something that feels like a bad idea. A leader listens to their internal compass instead. A leader has no need to prove themselves, and won't take on projects when they know they aren't the best person for the job.

They want their movement to succeed – so they support the best person for the job, instead of trying to do everything themselves.

#4 – Commitment

A leader can only lead by example. A leader can never expect others to be *more* committed to their cause than they are. Before a leader can be taken seriously as a preacher, they must first practice the changes they want to urge others to adopt.

Anything you are in charge of, you must model by example. If you want people to vote, to show up to city council meetings, or to do anything, you must first do it yourself.

When people see a leader who is genuinely committed to using their own lives to create change for the community, they will be inspired to do the same. If the people don't see any leaders leading by example, they will not be inspired to make change in their own lives.

#5 – Character

We hear often about "building character," but what exactly does that mean?

At the end of the day, character is the commitment to do what is right – no matter what the cost. It can mean giving up financial gains, personal comfort, and all sorts of other sacrifices. But we can only make progress as a society when leaders are committed to what is right for society – not just for themselves.

This may mean setting boundaries about what you will and will not do as a leader. Who will you accept as an ally or partner? What sorts of organizations are you willing to work with?

And, most importantly, how do you treat people? It's said that the way a person treats their enemy is a good measure of how they may someday treat their friends. So how will you behave when someone disagrees with you, or doesn't get onboard with your cause?

Here are some key-differences between people who have cultivated strong character, and people who are ruled by their emotions:

Character-Driven People	Emotion-Driven People
Do right, then feel good.	Feel good, then do right.
Driven by their commitments.	Driven by what's convenient.
Decisions based on principles.	Decisions based on popularity.
Actions control their attitude.	Attitude controls their actions.
Believe in it, then see it.	See it, then believe in it.
Create push to move forward.	Wait for push to move forward.
"What are my responsibilities?"	"What are my rights?"
Continue when problems arise.	Quit when problems arise.
Steady	Moody
Leaders	Followers

Now, which type of person do you want to be?

#6 – Identifying Your Team

Leaders don't do it alone. In fact, it's in the name! Leaders succeed by *leading people* – by organizing people to work collectively toward shared goals.

Picking the right team is one of the most important components of successful leadership. If a team has even one member who behaves abusively, irresponsibly, or selfishly, the team's whole effort may be sabotaged from within. One common anxiety of people looking for a cause to join up with is whether they will be able to rely on *all* the leaders and organizers to generally treat people well. So make sure *your* team is a team where people can expect that.

Leaders are most effective when they elevate others into a leadership mindset. True leaders are not people who claim all the power or glory for themselves – that *only* benefits themselves, and not their cause, community, or movement.

True leaders are those who empower the people around them. The most effective thing a leader can do to make change is to reproduce themselves. That is, to elevate *more* leaders who are just as capable of managing internal and external conflicts, and operating based on commitment and character, as they are.

This is the way real change happens: when a community is full of leaders who will not be swayed from the path of righteousness, unrighteousness cannot stand in their path.

Become a Fierce Leader

Leadership is something anyone can learn. It's not something that people are just "born with," or have to acquire by a certain age.

More importantly, our community *needs* all of us to be leaders. We cannot afford to sit back and be passive in the face of a racist prevailing culture and an entertainment industry which glorifies harmful behavior as "fun and cool."

Unfortunately, during the writing of this book, U.S. Congressman and iconic Civil Rights leader, John Lewis passed away from pancreatic cancer. He always said: "When you see something that is not right, not fair, not just, you have to speak up. You have to say something; you have to do something."

Congressman Lewis was and his words here are the epitome of leadership.

This book, my actions, and hopefully the actions of millions following this publication will produce the leadership necessary to guarantee social justice and progress for the Black community.

As we've seen in our examples above, just a small number of leaders can make a big difference. This is especially true when our leaders become engaged in building Black wealth and businesses, voting and putting pressure on lawmakers, and educating and entertaining the leaders of tomorrow in the right ways.

When each of us becomes a fierce leader who doesn't wait for permission, and who *also empowers other leaders*, we will be able to empower a fierce Black community to lead the nation and the world.

Chapter 6

Political Involvement:
Changing the Law

"I knew that I could vote and that that wasn't a privilege; it was my right. Every time I tried I was shot, killed or jailed, beaten or economically deprived. So somebody had to write a bill for white people to tell them, 'When a black man comes to vote, don't bother him.'"

-*Stokely Carmichael*

Did you know that the man who coined the phrase "Black Power" on national TV was also a fiery advocate of Black voting rights? Before Stokely Carmichael chose the black panther as the emblem of his own political party, he ran a voter registration campaign in Lowndes County where he managed to raise the number of registered Black voters from 70 to 2,600 in 1965.

This was significant because there were only 2,300 white voters in the county. Through his voter registration and political participation efforts, the county's Black population went from being totally unrepresented and unprotected by their government to being the *majority* of voters, winning county-wide elections, and making and repealing laws of their own choosing.

This is the power of the vote.

There was a time when our ancestors fought fiercely, risked their lives, and sometimes lost their lives, for the right to participate in politics.

Even before it was clear that the Civil War would end slavery, enslaved Black people saw the legislative differences between the North and South, and started making politically strategic moves to create a better future for their children.

When it became clear that Northern states contained strong movements supporting the abolition of slavery, Southern slaveholders began to panic. For many of them, their vast wealth depended entirely on their ability to legally own and force labor out of Black people. The enslaved people knew this, too: that's why many began to risk their lives to escape and offer help to Union troops as soon as the Civil War began.

One such hero was named Robert Smalls. Forced to work aboard a Confederate warship, Smalls and his fellow enslaved workers spent months learning everything there was to know about operating the ship, and the movements and routines of its white owners.

Smalls and his fellow Black workers waited until a cargo of large guns, canons, and ammunition were loaded onto their ship in an effort to deliver maximum benefit to the Union and maximum loss to the Confederacy. Then, when white staff disembarked from the ship and left the enslaved workers onboard, Smalls and his friends made their move.

First, they docked the ship and brought their families onboard. When the ship was filled with enslaved Black people, Smalls put on one of the captain's spare uniforms and began patrolling the deck, imitating the captain's distinctive way of walking.

Together, the Black crew sailed the Confederate warship through four Confederate checkpoints, successfully fooling guards at each checkpoint into believing that the ship was conducting a scheduled delivery of arms to another Confederate outpost. But when they left Confederate waters, the heroes weren't out of the woods yet. They now had to approach Union ships in a Confederate warship without getting shot at.

Fortunately, Union commanders found the approach of a single, lone Confederate warship to be suspicious – in a good way. Instead of firing on the ship they boarded it, where they found Robert Smalls standing at attention in his captain's uniform.

"I am delivering this war material, including these canons," Smalls said, saluting the Union officers. "And I think Uncle Abraham Lincoln can put them to good use."

When the Union began to lose the Civil War, Black Americans let it be known that they were powerful allies for the Union government. Half a million of them risked their lives escaping slavery and delivered themselves to Union military outposts where they hoped they would be allowed to help.

Unfortunately, the Union did not immediately allow these people to aid in the war effort. Still hoping to cater some goodwill among slaveholders, Lincoln did not free the slaves or pass laws allowing Black men to serve as soldiers in the Union army until it became clear that the Union had no other chance at victory.

When Lincoln finally did issue the Emancipation Proclamation – promising permanent freedom from slavery to any Black people who escaped the South or fought for the Union – the tide of the war immediately turned. With the help of the huge population of enslaved Black people who the South had forced to serve the Confederacy, the Union was able to become triumphant and the United States was preserved. But the fight for Black America was still not over.

With the newly re-unified United States secured, Black power became an asset fought over by white politicians once again. While some politicians did not want to give the newly freed Black population equal protection as citizens under the law, or allow them to vote, other politicians recognized that Black voters could make a powerful addition to their political party's power.

The fourteenth and fifteenth amendments increased the political power of the South, as Black people were now counted as a *full* citizen – not just 3/5ths of one – for Congressional representation purposes, as stated in the United States Constitution Article 1 Section 2. Politicians quickly realized that whoever could win the favor of Black voters would instantly gain tens of millions of votes in their favor.

For Black Americans everywhere, voting meant tremendous power. It meant the power to change laws that had once oppressed them, and pass laws that would help their communities. Black voters often chose to elect members of their own communities. In the first years after the Civil War ended in 1865, thousands of Black lawmakers were elected to city, state, and federal congresses. In Mississippi, Alabama, and Louisiana, former slaves now argued against their kidnappers and wrote laws to curtail their power on statehouse floors.

Robert Smalls himself was eventually elected to the U.S. House of Representatives. He is remembered today, not as a former slave, but as a war hero and a politician who fought ceaselessly to protect and expand the rights of his fellow Black Americans to vote, elect their own leaders, and govern their own communities.

Unfortunately, the suppression of Black votes began almost immediately after their right to vote was granted. Throughout the 1870s, Black people were murdered in attempts to scare other Black people out of voting in elections. "Literacy tests" – tests that people had to pass in order to vote, which could often be rigged or biased to prevent Black voters from qualifying – began to appear. When the last Union troops were withdrawn from the South in 1877, there was no longer any federal protection for Black voters in southern states.

In the century since then, many legal battles have been fought over Black voting rights. Though literacy tests have been outlawed – thanks mostly to Black activists and voters who fought against them – voter ID laws can now be used to turn away Black voters on suspicion of "fraud."

Although the Republican politicians who support voter ID laws today claim that the goal is to prevent people from voting more than once using fake names or identities independent analysts say that today's voter ID laws are "surgically targeted" at Black communities. Tactics like closing voting locations and holding elections on business days are also used to prevent people who have to work – most often people of color – from voting.

If our vote is so powerful and frightening that many white politicians are constantly seeking ways to stop us from voting, you might assume that Black people today are fighting just as fiercely for the right to vote and make laws as our ancestors in the past. Unfortunately, this is often not true.

In fact, today *most* Black Americans do not vote in every election that's available to them. Some try to vote and are turned away due to laws like the ones we've discussed above, but others don't feel that voting is worth their time, or don't even know when local and state elections are held.

All three of these factors – voter suppression laws, voter apathy and hopelessness, and voter ignorance – are carefully cultivated by the political enemies of Black communities to prevent us from taking control of our destinies.

If you don't vote, you see, politicians don't have to care how you feel about the laws they pass and the legal actions they take. If you don't vote, you don't pose any threat to them.

So how can we take back our voting power? How can we leverage the legal victories of our ancestors, and use them to make even more laws that create a better future for our children?

Steps to Social Justice & Legal Progress for our Communities

The year of 2020 has been nothing short of historic. It began with a global pandemic that has killed tens of thousands Black Americans as of June 2020 due to healthcare, housing, and income inequality that leaves our families more at risk than those of our white neighbors. In fact, according to CNBC at the time of this writing, Black Americans were dying of COVID-19 at three times the rate of white people.

Perhaps the pain our community is feeling due to pandemic losses is one factor contributing to the national unrest and riots in response to the senseless killing of George Floyd.

For those who are reading this book far enough in the future that you don't remember, George Floyd was a Minneapolis Black man who was murdered by a police officer on May 25th, 2020. Like so many Black people before him, Floyd was stopped on nonviolent charges – in this case, he was suspected of using a counterfeit $20 bill to buy cigarettes. The arresting officer kneeled on Floyd's neck for 8 minutes and 46 seconds while Floyd repeatedly pleaded: "I can't breathe." Nearby officers did nothing to help Floyd or stop the officer from asphyxiating him.

In the days after George Floyd's murder, it looked doubtful that any justice would be done. Since Black people are routinely killed by police without charges being filed or without even losing their jobs (in fact Derek Chauvin, the police officer who asphyxiated George Floyd had previously fatally shot three other people), the Black community realized that we had to respond.

The protests over Floyd's murder – which was caught on video – grew into the most widespread protests in American history. As of June 2020 while I am writing this manuscript, about 4,700 separate protests were happening across the U.S. each day. City councils across the country are scrambling to change their laws to appease the protesters.

The Minneapolis City Council has voted to dissolve its police department and rebuild policing from the ground up, to ensure that this never happens again. Its justice system has upgraded Derek Chauvin's charges from third degree murder to second degree murder (a more serious charge with more serious penalties) and has also charged the officers who watched it happen with aiding and abetting second-degree murder.

The San Francisco City Council has voted to create a team of unarmed emergency personnel trained in social work and respond to non-violent emergency calls such as welfare checks, mental health crises, and neighbor disputes in place of police. San Francisco has also voted to ban the use of military-grade weapons against civilians, and the hiring of officers with previous histories of excessive force or misconduct. Many cities across the U.S. have begun to pass similar laws in the space of a few weeks.

This is the power of protest.

It's worth noting that these votes are in most cases made possible by Black mayors and Black city council members who have been voted into power by the Black community. Without both Black voter involvement *and* protest, it's doubtful that we would be where we are right now.

Racism, injustice, and police brutality have existed for decades in our country. But with many instances now being documented and being shared millions of times on social media, millions of people have become outraged and are demanding change. As a result, it looks like change *is* slowly coming due to the massive uprising against these atrocities.

After an initially violent uprising, the majority of protests have turned non-violent because of the leadership of protest organizers and community leaders. Just as in the case in Minnesota with the murderers of George Floyd, other cases of police brutality are being reconsidered throughout the country.

This is a great development, but what must we do when we get the police reform we seek? What will solve our problems with police brutality and other challenges facing the Black Community?

To dive further into what should be considered, let's look at a quote from the great Dr. Martin Luther King Jr. regarding riots that occurred during the 1960s. Let's look at his *full* quote, instead of just the popularly used excerpt:

> "Certain conditions continue to exist in our society, which must be condemned as vigorously as we condemn riots. But in the final analysis, a riot is the language of the unheard. And what is it that America has failed to hear?
>
> "It has failed to hear that the plight of the Negro poor has worsened over the last few years. It has failed to hear that the promises of freedom and justice have not been met. And it has failed to hear that large segments of white society are more concerned about tranquility and the status quo than about justice, equality and humanity.
>
> "And so in a real sense our nation's summers of riots are caused by our nation's winters of delay. And as long as America postpones justice, we stand in the position of having these recurrences of violence and riots over and over again. Social justice and progress are the absolute guarantors of riot prevention."

I would like to humbly suggest that for decades, the Black community has not only rioted as a result of being unheard, but I dare to say the continuous criminal activity, however minor, is also a result of this voiceless feeling many have in the black communities across the country.

I agree with Dr. King's assessment that America has failed to hear the generational disgust of systemic racism that has continued to live well beyond his death in 1968.

There is absolute injustice in many areas in our country. We all know it's not just police brutality. As discussed in previous chapters, it's also income inequality, lack of access to better education, healthcare disparity, discriminatory lending, discriminatory housing policies, and financial illiteracy.

There are serious barriers to change that we all must pay attention to and become intentional about to forge change for years to come.

We cannot correct what we are not willing to confront!

If we begin to solve the issues of police brutality, the socio-economic inequalities will still be present.

White America isn't the only segment of American society who has not "heard" the plight of the Negro poor. I humbly suggest that even the more esteemed Black America has not "heard" the plight of the Negro poor fully.

We must admit this. We must hold ourselves accountable. We must implement a plan to be a part of this change we want to see.

Dr. King says that "social justice and progress" are the "absolute guarantors of riot prevention." And again I humbly add, "rioting" may very well include the crimes we now consider routine in many Black neighborhoods.

We must ask ourselves how we gain social justice and progress.

Everything rises and falls on leadership. People need to be led. It is *very* important that the individuals who already have influence step up and attempt to lead the way.

However, we cannot wait on them if they are not championing a high level of awareness and implementation strategy fast enough!

We must become leaders ourselves. Whatever voice you have you will need to use it and lead by example, as prescribed in the previous chapter.

If we really want change and are passionate about it, if we are able to coordinate our efforts, then we will see change brought about. But how?

Our leadership has to realize that the generations of solely religious propaganda, focus on athletics, and stylish culture have done nothing for our future generations. As poverty and inequality persist in the Black community, many talented and ambitious youth resort to illegal ways of finding "success."

We have already discussed the crucial roles played by the education and entertainment available to ourselves and our children; the financial literacy skills and practices that allow us to build real, lasting wealth; and the need for *true* leadership that teaches us to empower each other, not just ourselves.

One more crucial role is political involvement. We must pay attention, vote, and get most serious about local and state-level lawmaking.

We cannot do without this last step. Our votes are so powerful that politicians and billionaires scheme ceaselessly to take them from us. If we wish to build lasting change, we must use our powerful votes at every opportunity that arises.

There is great reason for hope now, as hundreds of thousands of people protest around the nation for an end to racist policing and other forms of racial inequality.

But there's only one way we're ever going to get the laws and funding that we need to fix forms of inequality like racist school funding policies, racist housing practices, and racist hiring practices.

We need to vote. Every single one of us. In every election that we can.

Most of you probably already vote in U.S. presidential elections. They're all we hear about on the news every four years, after all. But you might not even know the other types of elections and legislative bodies where you can make change. These include:

City Council and Municipal Elections

While the presidential campaigns get most of the media spotlight, the President doesn't have as much of a direct impact on the lives of citizens as you might think. Our local elected officials are the ones who dictate the local laws, policies and budgets that affect us the most, and these officials are being elected every year with little citizen involvement.

When was your last municipal or local election? Do you remember? I challenge you to take a moment right now to look up the date of the next one.

These elections have far more power over your life than you realize – and you have far more power over their outcome than you do over the outcome of national elections.

If you've spent most of your life focusing on national politics, you're not alone. Because national news channels usually don't cover local elections, it's easy for us to assume they are not all that important. But here are the top reasons voting for mayor, and your other local representatives, could mean the difference between creating the change you want to see or backsliding into inequality.

#1 – National Politics Starts With Local Politics

Just like all change starts in the home, all changes in national politics start with changes to local politics. If we don't have our house in order at the local level, we *can't* have it in order at the national level.

Indeed, that's one major reason why many politicians keep winning national elections – even with wildly unpopular policies and platforms. It's because they have mastered the art of focusing on local and state-level elections, allowing them to pass laws across cities and states that end up giving them control of national elections.

We can stop them from doing this. But only if we pay attention and get involved.

Generally, before a law is passed it must be voted on within your city council, state Senate and State House of Representatives. Then your mayor or governor decides to approve it, veto it, or allow it to pass into law. Laws passed at the city and state level are often used as trial runs or precedents for making national law. This means that laws often have to be passed at the city or state level before they have a chance at becoming national law.

This makes it extremely important to consider and vote for who your local elected officials will be, so that they will vote on your side. Our local officials are elected to represent the majority of *people who vote*. So whenever one of us fails to vote, we essentially send the message to our politicians that they can do whatever they want and we won't leverage our vote against them.

Increases in voter turnout at a local level can improve the representation of our communities in city councils and can improve the passing of laws that actually benefit our communities.

Has your community ever come up against a problem and been told that the law does not allow the government to help you? Have you ever faced a devastating problem *caused* by the law?

Municipal and state-level elections and council meetings are your chance to change that law. Learn how you can make your maximum impact by voting, campaigning, and showing up to meetings where the public gets a chance to make their voice heard today.

#2 – *Local Changes Have the Greatest Everyday Impact*

Local politics influence all of the decisions that determine our day-to-day lives. From the laws we're most worried about abiding by, to the paving and repair of the streets we drive on, to whether or not we'll have to pay for plastic bags at the grocery store – all of these are local laws.

Our local public servants use our property tax dollars to make big budgetary decisions for our communities, including education funding, welfare funding, local fines and zoning laws, and more. They're heavily involved in helping voters pass bills that often take precedence over national law.

One of the most prominent, recent examples of states dissenting from national law occurred when voters in Colorado, Washington, Alaska, Oregon and California made the use of marijuana legal, either medically and/or recreational. Although marijuana was still illegal at the federal level, the states knew that the federal government probably would not enforce federal laws that conflicted with state laws in this case. And they guessed correctly.

This reform, decided by local voters, had enormous local impacts in each state that created long-lasting effects on their economies, legal systems and more. People got rich running legal businesses, were released from prison, paid new taxes on marijuana that were used to fund local school systems, and were no longer fined or arrested because of these city- and state-level laws.

#3 – Policing the Police

Our local elected officials decide how our public safety is managed, how our police officers are trained, and how they themselves are policed.

As many of us know, use of lethal force and the Black Lives Matter movement are now at the forefront of most agendas nationwide. And while this is a national issue, it is city councils who actually have the power to determine the budgets and policies of the most powerful police departments nationwide.

City councils are now leading the charge on ending police brutality. The Minneapolis City Council has voted to completely dissolve and rebuild their police department, seeking to create a fairer, less aggressive way of responding to their citizens' needs. The New York City Council has voted to move $1 billion of funding from their police department into social services next year. The San Francisco City Council has voted to ban their police department from hiring officers who have track records of misconduct while working for other police departments.

(It's a bit worrying that this last law was not in place already, but in fact most cities have no rules against hiring officers with prior histories of violence or other misconduct. This is something we can change.)

Throughout all this, our national discussion has had little direct influence over how our local police departments behave, or in creating preventative solutions to reduce and respond to police brutality. In fact, the way the law is currently structured, *only* city governments can create Civilian Police Accountability Councils or make funding decisions or training policies for their local police departments.

If local citizens don't take action to make their voices heard, the interests of the majority cannot be met.

But when we do, the changes created can be dramatic.

#4 – Local Politics Help Shape Federal Policy

While the federal government has the ability to nullify any state laws that they disagree with and deem unconstitutional, they also choose their battles. If they don't see a law as worth the legal fight, they'll often step back to see how a new law plays out at a state level. This was the case with marijuana legislation, where states who legalized marijuana are currently serving as trial runs to see how legalization affects tax revenue, school funding, crime, and public health. If the results are good, the legislation could become national.

As states debate issues and reshape their laws, our nation may follow in implementing similar reforms over time. By electing local officials who support the causes you believe in, you can be part of making a change at a local level that could eventually catch on as federal law. And in the meantime, you'll be happy with the laws your city or state has incorporated, which often have bigger effects on your daily life than federal law.

Get In The Know. Get Involved.

Too often, voting is seen as something that occurs once every four years — and that needs to change.

Local elections are taking place every year, and their implications are long-lasting. To have a greater influence over laws in your city and state, start by staying informed on local issues so you can use facts to define your stance before you vote.

Your local city, county, and state government websites can help you keep up with the issues that matter to you the most, showing you both sides of each issue to help you make an informed decision, and giving you outlets to reach your local officials.

To stay informed on local elections, you can go to Elections.MyTimeToVote.com for important election dates by state.

This website will give you a short description of the different types of elections. You've probably heard of them: General, Primary and Caucus, Municipal, School and other Special Elections.

We have to stop making excuses about lack of opportunity, lack of information, lack of education, and figure out a way to create these opportunities and go after them relentlessly. We must become a community that is relentless in pursuing our best interests using the electoral and legal systems.

Unfortunately, many other races view the majority of the Black race as ignorant. This is of course because the "powers that be" have gone out of their way to hide information from us, to refuse to teach important information in schools, and to ensure that many of us grow up in the poorest school districts in the country, and further perpetuating this oppression through a focus on hip hop culture and athletics in our communities that is a far cry from the methods necessary for the majority of our people to gain progress.

This should make us angry enough to do something about it!

Use this anger as energy to inspire us to move to action. Rioting and committing crimes may make us feel like we have power and a voice, but these actions won't really help our communities.

Voting will.

There is no alternative. If we want respect and results, we have to earn it. As we can clearly see from American history so far, nothing will not be given to us without a fight!

We have this responsibility to our children and our communities. Otherwise, our future generations will not see progress.

If we want to become a REAL threat to a society that doesn't recognize our value and create real lasting change – this won't be accomplished by a man or woman with a gun, a brick, or other violence. It will be accomplished by a man or woman with a book, a computer, and a ballot.

The laws of your local city can affect the funding of public schools, prison sentencing, the legality of psychoactive substances, the creation or destruction of bus lines, subway systems, food pantries, homeless shelters, and more.

In short, the decisions of city council can transform life for you, your neighbors, and your children.

And the best part is, there's often fairly little competition to participate in municipal politics. So few people participate in city politics that the dedicated participation of you and your neighbors may turn the tide on important laws that affect your welfare and the welfare of your children.

We can do this, y'all. But we've got to do the work.

I know that's why you are reading this book. You are ready to help with and do the work!

That's why, right now, I'd like you to resolve to vote in your next local election. You may even wish to look to see when your next city council meeting is, and what issues will be discussed there. You may even be able to attend and tell your city council people how you really feel – and what they can do to get your vote in the next election.

After you've made a note of your next municipal election date, I challenge you to write down the phrase or type this up, print it out, and place it on your bedroom dresser mirror so you can see it each day before you leave home:

"I'm <your name here>, and I represent progress."

Chapter 7

The Power of Collective Action:
Working Together

"The ends you serve that are selfish will take you no further than yourself. But the ends you serve that are for all, in common, will take you into eternity."

- Marcus Garvey

It's not exactly a secret that there are divisions within the Black community. The loaded term "Black-on-Black violence," so often used by white people to claim that *their* violence against us doesn't matter, nonetheless refers to a real problem.

Many of our community members become wealthy and powerful. But so often, we use this power *against each other* instead of working together to build something greater.

It's easy to see why this might be tempting to do. When Black attempts to build collective power have been so frequently met with violence by whites, we can see why taking power from *each other* might be tempting. Fighting amongst ourselves over what little wealth and power we feel is available to us might sometimes feel like the *only* way to achieve individual success.

But that's exactly why we have to stop fighting amongst ourselves and start working together. *All* of us. When we fight amongst ourselves, we never increase the wealth and power available to our communities. We keep ourselves distracted from making real gains by simply moving what little we have around between different sets of hands.

And here's a news flash: that's exactly the way white supremacy wants it.

Way back in 1712, a slave owner named Willie Lynch delivered a speech to fellow slave owners. Lynch claimed to have a solution to all of the challenges experienced by slave owners in trying to keep their proud and resourceful Black slaves powerless and obedient.

Lynch's solution?

Simply turn the slaves against each other.

If they didn't trust each other or developed an "every slave for himself" attitude, there would be no more uprisings, rebellions, or even work strikes.

In Lynch's words, profit would go up because slave owners wouldn't even "lose stock" anymore by having to kill slaves who rose up as an example. Instead, when used properly, his technique would sow seeds of difference and distrust among slaves that would keep them powerless for hundreds of years to come.

What was Lynch's all-powerful tool? Simply a list of differences that could be found among slaves. West side and east side. Male and female. Hill and valley. Light-skinned and dark-skinned. All of these differences, Lynch explained, could be made into tools that slaves would hold against each other if they became convinced these differences were dangerous.

If you told male slaves, for example, that they could only be "real men" by violently controlling female slaves, they would spend their time and energy doing that instead of fighting against slavery. If you told slaves from the east side plantation and slaves from the west side plantation that they were in competition against each other for privileges and power, they would spend all their time fighting each other instead of the plantation owners who kept them in slavery. If you told dark-skinned and light-skinned slaves that they were threats to each other...

You get the point.

Is it possible that we're still acting out Willie Lynch's prescription for perpetual slavery in our communities today?

There have always been great unifiers in the Black community whose work and examples were so inspiring that they persuaded the tens of millions of American Black people to work together to fight for freedom, equality, and power. But all too often when these extraordinary figures pass away – or are assassinated, as the case may be – their movements fall apart.

We need to do better. We need to lead *ourselves* and organize *ourselves*. We need to focus on fighting the things that truly harm us – systemic racism, systemic income inequality, systemic lack of generational wealth – instead of fighting each other for the scraps that white supremacy allows us to have.

I want to take a moment to talk about one leader who unified maybe more Black people than anyone in history. Although some of his ideas were controversial and considered problematic by some of today's Black historians, Marcus Garvey was arguably *the* champion of the vision of a powerful, global black community in the late 19th and early 20th century.

Marcus Garvey and the Story of Race

As we discussed earlier in this book, white people started out divided amongst themselves. European kingdoms used to go to war with each other, expending millions of lives and the equivalent of billions of dollars in resources, for most of European history. But one day, a bunch of European leaders realized that they could build *more* wealth and power if they formed a common community. What did they all have in common? Their skin was pale compared to the rest of the humans in the world!

And so, the concept of the white race was born. With it came the concept of other "races" – huge consolidations of people from thousands of different ethnic groups, tribes, and nations, based vaguely on what they looked like. The idea that all white people – that is to say, all Europeans – should work together to extract wealth from these other people's lands created the basis for the biggest empires in the modern world.

Now, white people are not the only group to ever conquer or steal from someone else. They also aren't the only group to ever end up controlling a huge amount of wealth – the distinction of "wealthiest man to ever live" goes to Mansa Musa, a Black African king.

But white people consolidated wealth and power collectively more successfully than anyone in previous world history, thanks in part to their unifying under the pan-European banner of "whiteness."

In the 19th century, Marcus Garvey realized that the pan-African banner of "blackness" could be just as powerful.

Garvey was born in Jamaica, and later worked in various Central and South American countries. This experience gave him an advantage. He saw that the legacy of slavery and colonialism meant that Black people of African descent everywhere in the world outside of Africa tended to be racial minorities in their community who were often discriminated against and dominated by other races.

Garvey formed a bold plan based on this discovery: he felt that all Black people around the world should unite, return to Africa, and take their home continent back from the European invaders.

In the late 19th and early 20th centuries, this plan had a certain audacious genius to it. Black people all over the world heard their own experiences in Garvey's writings and speeches. Yes, they had been oppressed by colonizers. Yes, they did feel disenfranchised and threatened in the communities they lived in now. Wouldn't it be nice to go somewhere where they would be in the majority? Wouldn't it be nice to work together to *create* a majority of all Black people, everywhere?

Like Martin Luther King, Jr., Garvey got his start in organizing and gaining influence by working in pursuits that many modern people might find boring. His work as a union organizer gave him invaluable experience in creating real, concrete organizations of people that could take real, concrete action to fight for their own rights and interests.

He eventually founded the Negro Factories Corporation – an organization which sought to move real, material power into the hands of the Black Pride movement by organizing Black people who owned means of production – in addition to the Universal Negro Improvement Association and African Communities League (UNIA-ACL), commonly known as UNIA, which worked to determine how Black business owners, academics, and politicians could work together to solve all sorts of problems facing Black people, and the shipping company Black Star Line, which he hoped to eventually use to offer transportation to allow Black people in the Americas to return to Africa. The exact membership details of the UNIA is not known, but it has been said that by June 1919 it had two million members.

While some of his views and actions were controversial by today's standards (he sometimes spoke of "Black racial purity" and "returning Black people to Africa" in ways similar to the words of today's white supremacists, in the opinion of some historians), he may have been the most successful organizer in history to promote the ideas of Black Pride, Black unity, and a pan-African vision in which the numerous Black ethnic groups would work together to overthrow those who oppressed Black people everywhere and to do greater things than any single ethnic group or tribe could do alone.

Garvey's ideas influenced Martin Luther King, Jr., Malcolm X, and Nelson Mandela. All realized that cooperation was *so important* to consolidating any sort of wealth or freedom – and that Black people had to depend on *each other* for this unity in a racist global system. All of them also realized the importance of self-rule, rather than minority status, for Black communities in such a system.

Today, some view Garvey's name as tainted due to his belief in "Black racial purity" and his cooperation with white nationalist Senators who *also* wanted Black people sent back to Africa (they didn't seem to have figured out this meant they would lose access to forced Black labor). But the global scope of his vision and his determination to remove all illusions and obstacles which separated Black people from each other remains groundbreaking to this day.

Most of us today probably don't think of returning to Africa as the solution we want for our children (or maybe some of us do – several African countries are now inviting American Blacks to return to their ancestral homelands, and some are taking them up on it).

But that's the beauty of the global vision of Black unity.

Whether we live in the United States, Africa, or somewhere else in the world, Marcus Garvey's vision was that Black people would work together to build wealth, influence, power, and freedom. **Garvey's vision was one of a world where *all* Black people lift each other up, building a bigger and better global Black community.**

How to Initiate Collaboration

All great Black wealthy neighborhoods of our past started with, and were based on, successful Black collaboration.

From Mound Bayou in Mississippi in the late 1800s to Black Wall Street in the Greenwood community in Tulsa, Oklahoma in the early 1900s, Blacks have been very capable of building thriving communities and successful businesses!

It's unfortunate that over the last several decades, it feels like Back collaboration has dwindled and sometimes seems to barely exist. Maybe it is because of fear of white supremacist retaliation, deeply ingrained mental sabotage from society's messages to us, or a few other subjects we have discussed in this book.

Whatever the case, if we are going to progress as a community of people we must force ourselves to move past the oppressive efforts of others and the insecurities that have discouraged the kinds of collaborations that can build thriving businesses and communities, and which future generations can benefit from.

We need to do this to become examples for the current and future generations. If you are the first in your city to achieve success, that's great! But we can have *thousands* of grossly successful Black conglomerates if we follow these simple tips.

Let's take a look at 10 steps we can begin to build collaborations today:

Step 1: Establish Your Position.

Decide on and embrace what you are passionate about first. When you are naturally excited about something, that energy can be contagious when you find others who are like-minded and excited about the same thing!

Others can tell if you lack sincerity, so be honest with yourself about what excites you. This will lead you to knowing your strengths. And this passion and identity will set you apart from others as it gives you excitement that you can spread.

Step 2: Develop Your Message

Jot down a few sentences describing what you are passionate about and how you plan to enact change where you can. What solutions do you plan to work towards to solve the problems that plague our communities??

This way, you can communicate the value you could add to a team. This message reminds you what you work for every day, and communicates your role in community progress clearly to others.

Step 3: Network

It's time to get out and meet people. Even in the midst of a pandemic, you can still meet people virtually in different social media groups and virtual meetups. Search for these groups and meetups online, or on social media platforms. Watch for posts and events to engage with: these are where you will find like-minded people.

Attempt to build trust and relationships first before pitching anyone on your idea to change the world. This means getting to know someone, and becoming known as a reliable person and a doer. Listen more than you speak, and you will win friends and influence many. You will also learn a lot from people who may have been doing this longer than you.

Sometimes the process of letting people get to know you and learning the community can seem slow, but it builds up in big ways that can't be accomplished by simply rushing into a project with strangers too quickly.

Always remember, relationships create opportunities.

Step 4: Add Value

When you have an opportunity to engage with people or a group, look for ways to add value to the conversation. Be ready to have an answer if you are solicited about finding solutions, and contribute any relevant information or resources you may know.

Simply volunteering to spend a few hours researching a question or topic for the group may be seen as a big contribution and a sign that you are a reliable partner in business or community-building. Provided, that is, that you actually do your homework!

Be humble in your approach, but confident in what you can contribute. Seek to add something to relationships before you seek to receive any benefit. This will make your relationships so rewarding.

Step 5: Clearly Communicate Expectations

If you and a few others decide you will collaborate or there is a potential to do so, make sure at some point to decide on expectations of what the collaboration will look like.

What are the general rules about responsibilities? Are different people on the team responsible for different types of tasks and skills? How often will you meet, or how will you keep track of to-do items and deadlines?

The journey becomes easier and more exciting when everything is clear.

Step 6: Set Team Goals

Even before any agreements are written up, if the previous steps happen fairly quickly, you can start discussing what the goals would look like to further solidify everyone's confidence in working together.

You want to make sure that all the collaborators agree on the collaboration's goal, and how it will be measured. What is the concrete thing you want to accomplish? Is it measured in dollars? People subscribed to a mailing list, or showing up at an event? A quantity of donated items collected? A change to a law or ordinance?

If the decision has already been made, let's start putting goals on paper with target dates for completion in addition to specific directives for which individuals will be assigned what tasks to help accomplish the collective goals.

Step 7: Leverage Strengths

On a football team, everyone can't be the quarterback. There are eleven offensive positions on the field during a football game, and the quarterback is just one of them. In order for the team to function effectively, the other ten positions must be effective in playing their positions as best as possible.

Establish your strengths and your position. What are you best at, in terms of technical skills, specialized knowledge, and people skills? What sorts of resources do you have such as time, connections, etc.?. Which tasks does that make you best-suited to; with which tasks would you likely face challenges?

The focus shouldn't be on competing, but collaborating. The point is not to be the "star player," but to have a team so *full* of star players that no single team member stands head and shoulders above the rest.

Step 8: Foster a Culture of Accountability

We have all heard the term "Black Excellence." This should be more than just a cliche. We must develop a culture of excellence by holding each other to the highest of standards. We have so much to overcome to become successful as a community; the best way to train ourselves and our children for success is to encourage high discipline and excellent results from the individuals who seek to lead our companies and organizations. We must focus not merely on skills, but also on character.

If we hold each other accountable for how we do what we do, and for *who we are*, everything else will work itself out. By holding each other accountable, we will build the characters, minds, and communities that can do the impossible.

Step 9: Celebrate Each Other

Encourage *everyone* to get better and succeed, whether you work with them or not. We shouldn't have a mentality that we are competitors. Rather, we should have a mentality in which the successful lift up the rest. In that way, we *all* benefit from each others' success, and it makes sense for us to share seamlessly and praise shamelessly.

Even if we don't work together, we should create an ideal philosophy that each win for one person in our community is a win for us all. In this way, we will always be focused on seeing each other win in our community.

Step 10: Commit to Building Black Businesses

One constant complaint I hear about "supporting Black businesses" is the lack of customer service or seriousness some customers experience when doing business with them. Of course, these are flaws that any business can fall prey to. But we must be *especially* sure not to do so, because in a real way, each one of us represents the Black community in business or otherwise.

Many Black people don't know all of the ingredients of a great customer experience because many of us are first-generation entrepreneurs. So success has to be taught. And that doesn't just mean patronage and encouragement: it means accountability, discipline, and building character as well.

Always remember: we can't do what we don't know. So before you get upset with your fellow Black business owner because you feel you didn't get served at the level you felt you deserved, give them a chance by educating them or sharing your discontent to see if they would be willing to make it right. They might not even realize that they can do better, or how important it is that they learn.

I would have never become successful or produced millions of dollars from my businesses if I didn't make mistakes or make some people mad. I had to experience failure and some setbacks to teach me how to get better. My best critics were those who explained exactly *why* they were upset with me, and exactly *what* I needed to do to be better in the future.

We need to commit as a community to building up our Black businesses by not only "Buying Black," but also by encouraging growth and giving our fellow Black leaders the "benefit of the doubt" when things go wrong. We all learn fastest when we all behave as each others' mentors and mentees.

We need *us* to survive and thrive.

In most instances, "We are all we've got...but we are also all we need!"

A Way Forward

Our children will have both challenges and opportunities that we are just beginning to envision today.

They will have to cope with the environmental disasters and resource shortages caused by climate change and other forms of environmental destruction committed under colonialism. They will have to cope with a world that has a larger human population to support than ever before while its natural resources dwindle. They will have to deal with the economic fallout of the collapse of unsustainable ways of doing business and the cost of decades spent ignoring rising income inequality in the United States and around the world.

But when one door closes, another one opens. Our children will also have unprecedented *opportunities*.

They will have the opportunity to build a more sustainable, just, and kinder world using the advanced technology and understandings that they are already beginning to invent. They will have the opportunity to build economies that work *with* the most advanced principles of sustainability and well-being, instead of against them. They will have the opportunity to build societies based on consent, restorative justice, supportive community, and individual freedom in a way that the society we've had for the past few centuries just weren't.

They will have the opportunity to build a world like none we've ever seen before.

So let's empower them to do that. Let's work *together* to build generational wealth and change unjust laws.

Let's give our kids a head start on meeting the future.

Let's show them that WE, as a community of people, can pool our collective talents, collective finances, collective intellectual property, and collective action to create massive wealth for generations to come.

There is power in collective action! And we can do it!

Together.

Chapter 8

Finally – A True Plan for Our Reparations

"The three parties named will subdivide the land, under the supervision of the Inspector, among themselves and such others as may choose to settle near them, so that each family shall have a plot of not more than (40) forty acres of tillable ground, and when it borders on some water channel..."

> -*Special Field Order 15, issued by General William T. Sherman, US Army Commander*

You may have heard the expression "40 acres and a mule." This was a popular proposal for reparations that the government should grant to former slaves at the time the Civil War ended.

The logic was this: these people had, often for generations, been denied basic rights by the U.S. government. The basic rights they were denied included the rights to own property, and to own the wealth created by their own hands. Therefore, the government should compensate them in a way that would allow them to start building wealth immediately, now that they were legally allowed to keep what they created through their labor.

On January 11, 1865, Secretary of War Edwin Stanton arrived in Savannah, Georgia. His mission? To discuss with Generals Sherman and Saxton the crisis of Black refugees in the area, many of whom were former slaves with no land or possessions. Stanton and Sherman decided to consult leaders from the local Black community and ask them: "What do you want for your own people?"

On January 12, Sherman met with a group of twenty people, many of whom had been slaves for most of their lives. The Blacks of Savannah had seized the freedom of emancipation to strengthen their community's institutions, and they were eager for political power. They selected one spokesperson: Garrison Frazier, the 67-year-old former pastor of Third African Baptist Church. In the late 1850s, he had bought freedom for himself and his wife for $1,000.

Frazier spoke to his community and to many of the Black refugees in the area to determine their opinions before speaking with Sherman. He told Sherman: "The way we can best take care of ourselves is to have land, and turn it and till it by our own labor." Frazier suggested that young men would serve the government in fighting for the Union which had issued the Emancipation Proclamation, and that therefore "the women and children and old men" would be left to work the land.

Almost all of those present agreed to request land grants, to be used to create autonomous Black communities. This was deemed necessary on the grounds that racial hatred would prevent economic advancement for Blacks in mixed race areas.

Given Frazier's sentiments to General Sherman, the most straightforward way to do that was to give each newly freed Black family 40 acres of land and a mule with which to pull a plow. In this way, in theory, former slaves could begin growing and selling cotton or any other crop they pleased for their own use.

It would also have been an easy thing for the government to do: the federal government now controlled many formerly Confederate lands in the south, around the same time, the government was straight-up *giving* land away to any pioneers who agreed to settle and farm land out west through the Homestead Act.

Unfortunately, this didn't happen. The "40 acres and a mule" promise was never delivered on by the government in the South, and few slaves wanted to move thousands of miles from their homes, into dangerous territory where settlers often clashed with outlaws, to claim land. (Although some did: one little-known fact is that the real-life basis for the Lone Ranger was a Black man named Bass Reeves who became one of the most wildly successful lawmen in the history of the Wild West after escaping slavery.)

Black Americans aren't the only Americans who have fought for reparations from the U.S. government. American Indians, Japanese people who were forced into internment camps by the government during World War II, victims of forced sterilization, and victims of police abuse in Chicago have also demanded – and occasionally gotten – reparations from the government. These reparations have sometimes been transformative, but have often proven inadequate to remedy the harms done.

Examples of Reparations to Date

One instance in American history where the government has awarded reparations to Black Americans to compensate for the harm caused by white violence was in 1994. Florida became the first U.S. state to attempt to pay reparations to Black families who had lost lives or land to white violence in the previous century.

Unfortunately, the meagre $2 million set aside by the state for this purpose did not do much good. One woman – a descendant of a family whose farm was burned to the ground by a white mob 70 years earlier – received only $3,333.33 in compensation. While the government's admission of guilt and its apology was meaningful, the amount of money put aside was tiny, and would do the recipients little good without accompanying financial education.

Another attempt at reparations for Black Americans is currently being carried out by Georgetown University. After learning that the Jesuits who founded the school had sold of 272 enslaved Black people and used the profits to help pay for the school's founding, Georgetown students voted to increase their own tuition on the condition that the proceeds from the tuition hike would be paid to the descendants of those enslaved people.

The program is expected to raise about $380,000 annually in reparations for those 272 extended families. The school's board of directors has also agreed to give admissions preference to the descendants of those 272 slaves. Although the intentions are noble, one must imagine that the total benefit is hardly adequate compensation for an ancestor having spent their life in slavery.

For American Indians who sought reparations from the government, results have often been equally disappointing. Though several instances exist of the American government "giving" land or money to Indian tribes by way of compensation, the government has often declined to actually *give* the Indians these reparations.

Instead, they've done things like giving the Indians shares in a corporation that owns their ancestral lands, or placing reparations money into government-controlled trust accounts on the grounds that the recipients would not know how to use it well themselves.

There are signs of progress as a result of persistence. In 2012, the Obama administration agreed to pay $3.4 billion to settle a class action lawsuit filed against the government for mismanagement of American Indian reparations funds. Spearheaded by the tireless work of American Indian activist Elouise Cobell, who presented evidence that the government had often failed to make the payments owed to American Indians under the reparations acts and had instead pocketed the money for the government's own use.

President Obama welcomed the settlement and the billions in payment to the American Indians, but cautioned in his speech on the subject that this was in fact much *less* than they were rightfully owed after the wrongs done to them by the U.S. government. This case shows that the amounts being paid in reparations are getting larger, and there is a growing willingness within the political establishment to acknowledge that still more damages are owed for wrongs committed in the past which continue to affect people to this day.

So what can we learn about reparations from these well-meaning but often ineffectual attempts?

Reparations for the 21ˢᵗ Century

Even if the government decided to fulfill its promise of 40 acres and a mule to Black Americans today, it's doubtful that most of us would be thrilled about this. We no longer live in an era where anybody can build a log cabin with their own two hands and farming isn't the basis of most wealth.

So what *would* constitute "fair reparations" for the centuries of enslavement, Jim Crow, senseless murders, systemic oppression, and discrimination against Black Americans which continues to this day? What can help our households catch up to white levels of generational wealth, and overcome the uneven odds we often face in education, hiring, healthcare, and more?

A few ideas exist about the best way to compensate Black Americans for the damages of slavery in the modern era. I'd like to share with you two ideas to contemplate: one from Black billionaire Bob Johnson, and one from my own humble mind as a financial educator and servant leader.

Bob Johnson's Reparations Proposal

BET founder and Princeton graduate Bob Johnson has been vocal in his calls for reparations for Black Americans. The recent uprising led him to update and reiterate his call, proposing a $14 trillion plan that he hoped would level the playing field between Black and white Americans.

Johnson's argument that direct wealth transfer is what's needed. In his words, an infusion of wealth straight into the pockets of Black families who now own about 10% of what white families own on average, would compensate today's Black families for the wealth that was forcibly stolen from their ancestors. Johnson has called for Black business leaders and *all* business leaders to back this plan, which he acknowledges would be difficult to pass through our current U.S. Congress.

It's easy to see the appeal of this idea. With poverty often being a self-sustaining process, in theory a massive infusion of wealth could immediately put the Black families of today on the path to higher-quality education through private schools and prestigious universities, generational wealth through home equity, and other solutions that have been available to white families throughout American history but which Black families have often been denied.

However, Merck CEO Ken Frazier, who is Black, expressed doubts about this plan. According to CNBC, Frazier has gone on the record as saying that he doubts a plan like this would be passed by our current government, and that education and financial education are "the great equalizers."

I share his concerns. ***Wealth is, at best, half the battle in terms of what Black Americans have been deprived of in previous decades.*** It's an important and necessary component of security, but it's also something that we can grow – or lose –

according to our knowledge and specifically our financial education.

So how do we put Black communities in a situation where any wealth they receive through reparations will *grow*, doubling or tripling instead of disappearing over the course of a single generation?

I'd like to humbly propose the following plan for real, lasting reparations for the Black community. My hope is that this plan might be more acceptable to politicians *and* more sustainable as far as cultivating the skills and opportunities that will allow the Black community to grow wealth rapidly for generations to come.

F.R.A. Plan – Reco's Proposal for Real Reparations

While the idea of free money is nice, and can be life-changing for some, we've already covered some important reasons why this method of reparations might not be effective. If people have been denied knowledge about how to save, invest, and use other tactics such as property ownership, entrepreneurship, and investing in the economy to grow their wealth, even a fairly large amount of money can vanish quickly with no benefit for future generations.

In honor of Garrison Frazier, the Baptist minister selected to speak and presented the initial plan for reparations for the Black community in 1865, I humbly present my plan for real reparations that will guarantee social justice and progress for the Black community: *The Frazier Reparations Act*:

#1 – Billions to Provide Financial Education for Every Black American

We've already spoken of the power of a world in which we each grow up knowing how to build, manage, and grow wealth. By entering adulthood with a key eye for finance, we could grow our wealth to be double or triple what we would otherwise achieve. We could pass on that wealth – and those skills – to the next generation, and to every generation after that.

That's why I propose that a portion of the reparation money be used to create financial education courses and programs that should be made available free of charge to all Black adults and children. A combination of online courses and in-person community courses administered through schools and churches could transform the mindset, knowledge, and wealth-building potential of this and future generations. It could change our narrative. Not only how the world sees our community, but more importantly how we see ourselves!

The cost to execute this plan successfully would, of course, be in the billions of dollars. And we mustn't skimp on this essential component of the plan to build generational Black wealth. Let's ensure that Black businesses receive the billions that they need to provide every Black person in this country with engaging, high-quality financial education that will have a lasting impact on their narrative for generations to come.

As the saying goes: "Give a man a fish, you'll feed him for a day, but teach a man to fish and you'll feed him for a lifetime."

Instead of giving out "free" money and giving Black people temporary wealth, we need money to teach the Black community to fish so they can gain high-yield investments and wealth for a lifetime. Helping current Black businesses and other Blacks who want to become successful in business is the key to generational wealth in our communities.

#2 – Reduced Credit Score Requirements for Business Loans

We've already spoken in this book about the importance of business loans. The ability to borrow $10,000 or $20,000 at a low interest rate is today's business equivalent of 40 acres and a mule in the late 1800's. It's the ability to buy equipment, pay rent on a storefront, pay employees, and meet any other number of essential needs to turn a great idea into a highly profitable business.

Too often in the modern world, Black entrepreneurs are denied business loans. Part of this is straight-up discrimination, and that's hard to fight legally. But a big step forward would be lowering the credit score requirements imposed by the government, banks, and businesses when it comes to Black applicants.

"But Reco," you might be thinking, "how would this help?"

Well, for reasons we've covered in this book, Black individuals often struggle with credit more than white individuals. This isn't our fault. It's an effect of systemic poverty, discrimination in housing and hiring, lending and interest rates, poor healthcare, denial of financial education, and any other number of factors that make it harder for Black families with a national average net worth of $17,500 to pay the bills compared to a white family with a national average of $171,000 in assets and savings.

If you take financial hits from discrimination at every turn, of *course* you're going to have unpaid bills. Or you may never have been taught to open up credit lines *at all*, resulting in you effectively being punished for paying your bills without borrowing money to do it.

How do we solve this? By giving Black business owners a chance, even if their credit scores aren't perfect. Simply by increasing access to business loans by changing credit score requirements, we can ensure that more Black entrepreneurs get a chance to succeed. I propose that Black business owners receive a 100 point concession relative to what their non-Black counterparts require to qualify for business loans.

For example, if the minimum score needed is 680 to qualify for the loan, Black business owners can qualify with a minimum 580 credit score. *This and other concessions would be reparations for the years of oppression faced by the Black community.*

#3 – Reduced Credit Score Requirements for Home Loans

Home loans are to the family what business loans are to businesses. One major benefit afforded to many whites across the course of history has been the benefit of home loans backed by major banks or the government. For much of American history, these institutions *wouldn't* back home loans for Black families, fearing the wrath of racist politicians and voters who didn't *want* Black families to get an equal chance at building wealth, or at becoming their neighbors.

In some ways, credit scores are one way in which generational poverty has become self-perpetuating. If your parents couldn't keep the bills paid because of housing or hiring discrimination, your family may have been denied the chance to own a high-value home which could accrue more wealth for your family over time. Now is the time to change that.

That's why one small step toward racial equality would be lowering the credit score requirements for Black families applying for home loans. In this way, we can have expanded access to what so many white families have had all along: a chance to purchase a high-value property that will build wealth for our families for generations to come. I propose that Black families receive a 100 point concession relative to what their counterparts have to possess when being considered for home loans and mortgages.

#4 – *Grants for Black Family Businesses and Black Children's Education*

Some of you may know that the government is in the business of giving grants. If they decide that an activity is in the government's best interest – for example, going to college or starting a small business or nonprofit that fills a certain need – it may give you a few thousand dollars, or a few tens of thousands, to help make the process easier.

One interesting finding of 20th century economists has been that *all* of America suffers when Black families and businesses suffer. In fact, Black economist Dr. Lisa Cook has estimated that the United States has lost the equivalent of the GDP of a small European country as a result of denying Black people the best in legal protections, education, and business opportunities.

Now is the time to start fixing that. Government grants to support Black home loans, business loans, college education, private school tuition, etc. would allow the Black students and entrepreneurs of today to immediately start competing on a level playing field – and we could all sit back, relax, and watch our GDP skyrocket as a result.

It is important to note, there needs to be a few requirements. For business owners who have an active listing with their Secretary of State, EIN filed with the IRS, and business bank account, but there shouldn't be underlying rules that make it difficult for these business owners to gain immediate access to the capital when applied for. If a simple list of items are checked off, approval should take place in a matter of days. This grant should be at least $25,000.

Black high school graduates that graduate with at least a 3.0 should be granted $25,000 in grant money towards the college of their choice to cover ANY college expenses.

#5 – *Reduce Fees and Taxes on Black Families*

What's a *really* easy way for the government to make up for the wealth our ancestors were not allowed to keep? Well, the lowest-effort way the government can address this is to simply cut back on the amount of wealth it takes from us today.

Lower fees and taxes for Black families would go a long way toward making up for generations of wealth inequality, all without requiring the government to actually "give us" money. Simply cutting our federal and state tax rates and fees for items like business licenses – say, by 90% in concordance with the wealth difference between the average Black and white household – would make it literally an order of magnitude easier for Black families to start saving, investing, and succeeding.

This measure would also motivate Black achievement. Instead of giving us free money, the government would be making it much, much easier for us to start profitable businesses, and motivating us to earn more by allowing us to keep more of what we earn. Trickle-down economics may not work when taxes are cut exclusively on millionaires, but if you drastically cut the tax rates on a low- or middle-income family or entrepreneur, you can bet their incentive to earn and keep money *will* increase.

#6 – *Billions for Underserved "Majority Minority" Schools*

As we have discussed, our unequal school funding system, combined with housing and hiring discrimination, is one of the major culprits in the suffering of the Black community today. By linking public school funding to property taxes, the government ensures that students of already-rich families receive the best education, while students of impoverished families may effectively receive no education at all.

One term used to discuss what is effectively modern-day segregation is the term "majority minority." The idea is that if a school or county is composed *mostly* of people who are a minority in the overall population, there is probably some form of segregation going on.

It may not be official – it may be accomplished through historical and current discrimination, rather than straight-up banning members of a certain race from certain neighborhoods or schools. But the result is the same: these statistically unlikely situations show that some serious racial discrimination is at work.

Unfortunately, "majority minority" counties and schools today account for a *vastly* disproportionate percentage of poor outcomes. Just 22% of American counties are majority Black, yet these 22% of counties have accounted for *60%* of U.S. COVID-19 deaths as of this writing. While just 7% of white Americans struggled with basic reading as of 2003, *24%* of Black Americans did. The underlying root causes of systemic poverty and discrimination are the same, whether we're looking at educational or healthcare outcomes.

The ideal solution to this problem would be to ban discrimination in school funding. How do we do that? By disconnecting public school funding from property taxes, and instead requiring that every school receives *equal funding per student* at the state level. This system would allow for some variation in regional cost of living without punishing the children of low-income families for being born into poverty.

In such a system, better education for some students would require funding better education for *all* wealthy families wishing to increase their child's school funding would be forced to increase funding for *every student in their state* at the same time.

This is a proposal that not just Black neighborhoods, but voters in *all* low- and middle-income neighborhoods could get behind. The parents of arguably *most* students could expect their school budgets to rise if money were distributed equally per student instead of according to the size of their parents' home and paycheck.

And wouldn't it be worth it for *all* of us to live in a better-educated, more productive society? When school districts are funded equally for the rich and the poor alike, *every* child in America will have a more equal shot at becoming the next Robert Smith (a man whose success was only enabled by his wealthy school district's early access to computers, by the way). Imagine how much our GDP will rise then!

Unfortunately, this solution may be difficult to pass into law because of the role played by money in politics. Extremely wealthy campaign donors may hesitate to support politicians who may want to take some funding from their extremely wealthy neighborhood schools and give it to impoverished schools within the same state. This is where political participation comes in: *we* can vote, campaign, and donate to politicians who *do* support our views. Between us, we surely outnumber the billionaires.

If such a proposal truly can't be passed in our state and national legislatures by an agreed upon deadline no later than the year 2022 an alternative should be implemented to provide billions in funding to school districts with 60% or more Black students. This measure would benefit fewer Americans and would likely not have the same long-lasting effects as requiring equal funding per student at the state level, but it might be more achievable in the short term for the very reason that it would be a more modest redistribution of funds applying only to Black school districts.

Either way, it is essential that we take action to procure billions of dollars for the schools that are so frequently dismally underfunded, and which so frequently leave our students feeling that academic and career success are not realistic goals for them.

#7 – *Billions for Black Scholarships*

Every Black family knows that the cost of a college education can range from "intimidating" to "terrifying." Too many brilliant Black children forego college simply because it's not feasible for them or their families to pay tuition for the prestigious institutions they could be admitted to. While grants and scholarships do exist, they are so few and far between that Black students are still drastically underrepresented on college campuses nationwide.

Student debt is a problem we are grappling with at the national level, since Americans now own more in debt for higher education tuition than they owe on all their credit cards put together. But until a solution is found that makes college affordable for all Americans, it's imperative that we make it affordable for the brilliant Black children who may otherwise avoid school simply because it is too expensive.

To this end, I would propose a simple fee reduction for Black students. Perhaps a 90% fee reduction on up to $100,000 in tuition for undergraduate and graduate schools – reflective of the average wealth disparity between Black and white families – would be a fair and simple way to allow our young people to develop their skills and abilities to their fullest potential without breaking the bank.

Call this a scholarship if you like. Call it having the government cover the cost, or call it simply waiving the fee. The important thing is, this would put a decent college education within reach of every single Black student who felt that college or graduate school was their true calling.

Moving Forward on Reparations

One may ask, "Reco, who is going to cover all the risks taken on by these credit score concessions and loans that are given that may not be paid back?"

Well, the government is going to cover that risk, just like it covers the risk and regularly bails out major national corporations. That's why this is a part of the reparations plan! It allows for government assistance in the event of a catastrophe, but the even better part is this:

If the loans don't default and are paid back with interest, the "Reparations Fund" is continued into perpetuity. The money that's been paid back to the government with interest is now available for future Black businesses and families to borrow. Just like the businesses that rise as a result of Wall Street, all of this would be government-backed whether it is a success or failure.

As we've already seen, getting politicians to pass *any* reparations plans at all has been difficult. Those that are passed are often inadequate or poorly designed to meet the true needs of the community.

That's why my proposal incorporates both spending and non-spending options. Lowering credit score requirements for business loans and buying homes doesn't cost the government a cent, but it could make us and the government billions if we play our cards right. But we must also allocate the money in the right way, and focus on educating the Black community properly to handle this newfound opportunity.

Waiving or reducing fees such as taxes, business licenses, and college tuition may cost some organizations revenue, but the incurred losses should be tax deductible so that the perceived "loss" is not a true loss at all.

Using what precious money we are granted through these reparations for financial and academic education will ensure that the change we make lasts generations.

So what do you think?

Can we mobilize the Black community to demand that some of these proposals be signed into law?

Can we show up at the voting booth and vote in politicians that support these and similar proposals at the city, state, and federal levels?

If none of them are willing to do it, can we put together some petitions or maybe even run for office ourselves?

We are some of the brightest, fiercest, toughest positive hustlers in America today. And there are almost 50 million of us in the American Black community.

Together, we can get this done for sure!

Chapter 9

Let's Do This!

"It always seems impossible until it's done."
-Nelson Mandela

I want to thank you for taking the time to read this book. Reading this book represents an investment in your community. Now that we know the steps we must take to accomplish lasting social justice for our children, grandchildren, and future generations to come. We can go out there and do it.

Remember: your skills are the most powerful asset that you have. Investing in your own skills and knowledge is the best investment that you can make. I'm excited and humbled that you've decided to give me the chance to share what I know, so that we can all prosper together.

Those of you who know my story know that I come from humble beginnings. As a child, my family's electricity would sometimes get shut off. I didn't even realize what was happening until I was much older: my mother would proudly proclaim that we were going "indoor camping," and make such a special event of these electrical outages that I remember them as an adventure.

But now, I realize the truth. Like so many of us in the American Black community, I came from poverty. I came from a deeply unfair circumstance, created by the systematic exploitation of my ancestors and the theft of the wealth they created. I was blessed with a mother who taught me the right mindset, and that turned everything around. Today my family is on the road to wealth and power that will last for generations.

We can do the same for our children. We can do the same for ourselves. But we can't do it alone. Emma Lazarus, who composed the poem inscribed on the Statue of Liberty's pedestal, also made famous another quote: "Until we are all free, none of us are free."

Individual success is not enough to ensure prosperity and freedom for our children.

That's why I'm asking you to join me in doing the work to make this vision a reality. We can leave our children a much better world than the one we inherited – but only if we do the work.

This probably sounds intimidating. There are many steps covered in this book, and many aspects of the problems that perpetuate Black poverty. The work will involve a lot of learning, a lot of growing, and a lot of forging new relationships in our community.

I was blessed with a mother who knew that everything was possible with God and the right *mindset*. When we wake up in the morning excited about what we can achieve, as Nelson Mandela said, we can do the impossible. Even the Bible tells us that Jesus said in the book of Matthew, chapter 19, verse 26 that "with God, all things are possible." But the Bible also tells us that "faith without works is dead," which means if we don't do the work, the faith in God is useless.

So how do we keep up that excitement to do the work? How do we wake up, day after day, excited about what we are able to achieve? This can feel particularly frustrating when the process is slow. We can't simply *will* social justice into existence. We must spend years learning and working with both patience and persistence to see lasting results that will benefit our children.

So how do we stay excited about that every day? That's what this chapter is all about.

If you don't believe in something, you're not going to give it all you've got. You're not going to be able to get excited about it and work on it obsessively.

With the tactics below, you can shift yourself from a mindset of pain to a mindset of power.

I encourage you to take notes on this chapter. Reread this chapter as often as you need to. You need to believe in yourself 24/7. Some of the tactics here might be very different from the way you're used to living, but that's good! It's how you know they really will change the status quo if you put them into action in your own life.

As you do this work, don't compare yourself to other people. Compare yourself to yourself. As long as you're getting better, you're moving in the right direction.

The secrets below are used by high-performing businessmen and entrepreneurs to make millions. Making millions is only a small part of the whole-system picture of social justice for the Black community, but the same methods that can turn poverty into riches can also accomplish any other goal you set your mind to.

#1 – The Power of Community

Ideas and emotions are contagious. This is very powerful. For better or worse, you are likely to pick up the habits, beliefs, and overall life situation of the people you spend the most time with.

When we use this to our advantage, it is incredibly powerful. A person can pick up new skills every day simply by spending time with people who already have them. They can do things they would never have been able to do alone, simply because they are surrounded by role models and encouragement.

When we ignore this principle, it can prevent our success. When we are convinced that we can bootstrap ourselves to our goal without teachers, mentors, co-conspirators, and supporters, we nearly always fail. This is just a fact of life.

You might be telling yourself that *you're* different – you can have success without having to spend time around people who are also dedicated to the same goal you are. I strongly caution against that mindset.

The good news is, this is work that we have to do together as a community anyway. "Until we are all free, none of us are free." That's why I recommend that, whether you've set your sites on changing the law or on making a million dollars, you surround yourself with a supportive community. Peer mentoring and accountability partners are the bread and butter of entrepreneurship, and the same is true for social justice work.

If you have to, share this book with a friend. Share it with ten friends. Start your own social justice network. Start going to meetings of groups dedicated to these goals which already exist.

People that work for social justice together stay excited together.

You also may ask, "What if the people around me are not willing to do what it takes to succeed or are not willing to put in the work to change?"

My answer to you would be that if you want to change your life, and your friends are unwilling to change with you, then you need to change your friends.

Let me say it another way: *If you can't change your friends, change your friends.*

#2 – Win In Your Mind First

No obstacle is too large if you can master this technique.

You might think it's corny when people tell you to visualize success. Some people think of this as wishful thinking, or some New Age idea. But here's a secret: virtually *all* of the highest performers in the business world do this. Virtually all of them agree that it is *necessary* to do this.

And this is a tool that's available to us for free, every day. So how does it work?

With visualization, you create a crystal-clear vision of what victory looks like.

What would it look like, for your kids to have access to the very best public schools in the country? What would it look like to live in a world without prisons, where Black communities are no longer devastated by drugs and incarceration? What would it look like for your city council to repeal the laws that are harming the people, and fund the resources that they need? What would it look like for your children to be heirs to the kind of inheritance that will give them an advantage everywhere they go?

Visualize the details clearly. What does the air smell like? Who is there, and who is smiling? How did you do it? What can you do now that this vision is accomplished?

Spending time in this vision at the beginning of every day will automatically shore up your commitment to do the work that needs to be done. You will start your day excited and energized about the future that *is* possible – just ask Nelson Mandela about dismantling Apartheid, a system of harsh segregation in South Africa in the mid-to-late 20th century.

#3 – *Box Breathing*

Breathing exercises are another powerful ally to these visualization exercises. Scientists now know that the way we breathe actually changes our brain activity. The benefits of "diaphragmatic breathing," as the medical community calls it, are so great that clinical trials are seeing improvements in everything from asthma to open heart surgery outcomes as a result of breathing exercises.

People who operate at a high level perform visualization and breathing exercises every morning as a way of "hacking" their brains and their performance. This is just a fact. It really works.

The type of breathing I'd like to tell you about here is called "box breathing." It heightens your performance and concentration, so it's a good idea to practice it in the morning along with your visualizations.

Box breathing goes like this:

1. Slowly exhale. Sit up straight and breathe out slowly, getting all the oxygen out of your lungs. You may notice that your abdominal muscles contract more than they usually do to expel all that air. That's good! That's exercise.

2. Slowly inhale. Breathe deeply in through your nose while counting to four. You may notice that your lungs and stomach are filling up with air more than they usually do.

3. Hold your breath. Slowly count to four while your lungs remain full.

4. Slowly exhale again. Remember to sit up straight and let all of the air gently leave your lungs.

Ready for a life-changing performance hack? That's it. Really. The change in your breathing will strengthen your breathing muscles, release stress, and change your brain activity in a way that's compatible with concentration, confidence, and excitement.

After ten minutes of visualizing your goal and box breathing, you are ready to go for a winning day of getting the work of social justice and progress done!

This might sound really strange and foreign to you. Again, that's great! If you want to accomplish something new, guess what? You've got to start doing something new, too.

One theme we will encounter often here is that, to grow your abilities and your achievements beyond your wildest imagination, you will have to get comfortable being uncomfortable. Rapid change is always uncomfortable, and change is what we need. At the personal, community, and national level.

The secret of box breathing is that it actually interferes with the physical processes that are causing pain and doubt. By changing your brain activity and your body's movements, it is deconditioning the trauma you have experienced from the effects of racism in the U.S. and many other emotional and physical ailments you may be dealing with at the moment.

When you take your breathing and your visualization into your own hands, you take your destiny into your own hands. You start seeing yourself as a winner.

I remember visualizing where I am now back when I was living in a one-bedroom apartment. Many people around me told me that it wasn't reasonable for me to expect to make millions of dollars, yet here I am. And I'm now able to use this platform to do my best to educate and inform you, so that you can experience success – whatever 'success' might mean to you.

In time, you will build confidence born of experience as a result of this practice. When you go into the world inspired, you will try new things and experience small successes. You will find victory in small daily wins with grace and humor. That will all work to keep your excitement, and your enthusiasm for the mission, up and running.

When you see yourself as a winner daily, you build the power, confidence, and self-possession that CEOs and politicians have. You *become* that person who feels he or she can do anything!

Do this daily. Just 10 minutes a day. See how it changes the way you see yourself, the way you act, the way you feel.

The people who don't do this are the ones who will never get to their destination. They will be the ones left feeling that our goals are unrealistic or hopeless. You've got to overcome the negative self-image that has been conditioned into you by a racist society.

Some days you won't believe in yourself, and that's okay. That's important to know, too. We all have off days. Just because you don't feel up to speed one day doesn't mean your whole future is shot.

When you wake up feeling hopeless, *do this morning practice anyway*.

Slowly, over time, you will uproot your doubt and pain at its source.

You must relentlessly move forward toward success in your goals. And I mean *be relentless*.

Research. Learn what you need to know, who you need to know, and what you need to *do* to reach the next step toward your goals.

Practice your breathing. Visualize. Affirm. BELIEVE.

Your own internal state, yourself, is the greatest asset you have. If you ignore yourself, if you ignore your own mental state, if you don't try to better yourself and your mental state, you won't get anywhere.

Think of your bad days like potholes in the road. They exist, they happen from time to time, and they can trip you up. But you can learn how to fix them, and even how to avoid them.

Learn your own inner landscape. When you find something inside you that stands in the way of your goal, repair it. Gently and lovingly – but relentlessly.

#4 – *Affirmations*

As you condition your mind and body to be in a place of free-flowing energy, it is important to start speaking things that have not yet come to pass, as though they already are. We call this exercise "affirmations."

This is another hack for getting to success that the greats do daily. Adversity is not only faced by unsuccessful, poor individuals; it's faced by the very wealthy and highly successful as well. The difference is how the successful handle adversity. They believe: "It is not what happens to me that determines my destiny. It is how I react to what happens to me that determines my destiny.

To that end, successful people visualize what they want then start speaking that reality into the atmosphere. Seriously. They say it out loud and even in the mirror, until what they visualize and desire comes to life.

For example, when I first started my entrepreneurship journey, I didn't have much money. To put it another way, I was broker than the Ten Commandments. I went to a seminar and a very wealthy man was speaking and he said: "The reason why most people are broke is that they are always talking about it and saying it."

I want you to think about that for a moment. When someone asks you to do something and it may be outside of your budget, do you say: "I'm broke, I can't do it?" Or do you constantly think to yourself that you are tired of being broke?

Whether you know it or not, you are placing yourself in a perpetual state of remaining broke, because being broke consumes your thoughts. If you identify yourself with lack, then that's what will continue to manifest itself in your life: lack.

If you want to prosper in your life, in all areas, you must change your identity and what you believe for yourself.

For me, instead of continuing to proclaim I was broke, I decided I would get up every morning and proclaim I was rich! I began this practice the very next day after leaving that seminar.

Each morning thereafter I would wake up and say a quick prayer. Then I'd go to the bathroom, look at myself in the mirror, and say: "Good morning, Millionaire!"

I'd like to remind you, this day and many days after that morning, I had less than $100 in my bank account. But that is how I greeted myself each morning, and the morning after that. "Good morning, Millionaire!"

Day after day, week after week, month after month: "Good morning Millionaire!" I was conditioning myself to arrive at what I started believing for my life. And guess what happened?

One day I woke up and I was a...*hundredaire*! LOL!

We all have to start somewhere. You don't go from broke to millionaire status overnight. But at least my net worth was positive now, which by the way, many people in this country lack. So I continued my affirmations, each morning. "Good morning, Millionaire!"

Eventually I became a THOUSANDAIRE!

What was happening during these affirmations each morning was that I started BELIEVING I was a millionaire, even before the money showed up. Since I started believing it, I felt good about my direction and what I was doing. My actions became more intentional, because I was confident.

So morning after morning, I would continue: "Good morning, Millionaire!"

And you guessed it – one morning I woke up, and I arrived at what I envisioned! But I didn't wait for it to show up. I spoke it into existence!

You must do the same. Not only in terms of the money you would like to earn, but also in your relationships, your health, your fight for social justice and progress for our community. Any and everything you desire to have in your life, first starts in your thought life!

This is why it's so vitally important to take time to visualize what you want, get your mind and body right, and to say that it is so. Over time, you will see that you become a different person. The person who you want to be.

Always remember, what you think will determine how you feel, and how you feel will determine how you act. How you act will determine the results that you get in your life. So the first four tips here create your thought life, and this is the foundation for your personal success and also the success of THE PLAN that will guarantee social justice and progress for the black community!

The major takeaway here is that in order for you or anyone to get something to appear in the physical world, on the outside, we must first believe it and visualize it on the inside. This principle is powerful and will serve you well for the rest of your life. Guaranteed!

#5 – Be Fanatical About Your Mission In Life

We all know a fanatic. Someone who shapes their entire life around what they believe. Many fanatics describe having an "aha" moment: the moment they realized that this was what life was all about, so why do anything else?

This is the kind of belief that leads to real change. When we change everything about our lives in ways that make our lives – and our communities – better, we can transform the world.

I said earlier that you need to find others who believe in your mission in order to go far. But you don't have to care about what other people think. The best entrepreneurs and the most astounding activists are repeatedly told by their teachers, their peers, and sometimes even their families that they're crazy. "That will never work."

But they know better. They have knowledge that the others don't. They have *belief.* And next thing you know, that "crazy, impossible" thing is the next big thing that's shaping our world.

If you're an ambitious Black person, you may have been told that real change and power are not possible for you from many sides. From teachers and peers who may feel you're setting your sights too high to a hip hop culture that often limits its success stories to those of athletes and entertainers, you may have been told that obtaining that degree, changing the school system, changing the prison system, and changing the law are unrealistic goals.

Don't believe it. Form a belief in your community of co-conspirators that's so fanatic no one can talk you out of it. This will inspire you to change everything about your lives – and start a change in society along with it.

This can be compared to being grounded and rooted in religious belief. You know how that story goes. Someone tries the religion's beliefs or practices and finds that their life gets better. When they decide they want to pursue that improvement for everyone, everywhere, their whole life changes. They become capable of incredible things.

You can do the same. People of all religions, or none at all, can crusade for social justice.

After all, isn't that the first teaching of every faith? "Do unto others as you would have them do unto you."

And that means fighting for freedom for all people, everywhere. The Black community in America is especially in need of freedom fighters right now. The whole world will be soon.

You know what you know. You know what's fair and what's not. And I hope you know, after reading this book, a little bit about how to change what isn't fair.

So let's become freedom fanatics. Together.

#6 – Fail Forward

Many of us don't act because we're afraid of failure. We're afraid of screwing up. But, newsflash: everyone screws up. *Especially* successful people.

The term "fail forward" has been circulating in the business community in recent years. It's a reference to the fact that *most* businesses – and most attempts at doing anything worth doing – fail.

That can sound disheartening. It's not! Remember, it only takes *one* success to overturn an unjust law or catapult an entrepreneur to riches. The knowledge that it's *normal* and *necessary* to fail before we succeed is incredibly empowering.

We are often told to avoid mistakes at all costs. The truth is, that's a mindset for servants. It's a mindset for people who are expected to be obedient, convenient, and helpful. Who are expected not to cause problems.

It's not a mindset for people who are expected to change the world.

The late great U.S. Congressman John Lewis said it best at the Bates College commencement ceremony in 2016: "Go out there, get in the way, and get in trouble. Good trouble. Necessary trouble!" He went on to say "You have a moral obligation, a mission and mandate, when you leave here, to go out and seek justice for all. You can do it. You must do it."

Unshakeable belief in yourself and your goals comes from experience. You can't *get* that experience, however, if you don't try. You also can't get it if you give up the first time you get yelled at or make a mistake.

Instead, to gain a true understanding of what is possible, it's necessary to try *relentlessly*. It's necessary to keep trying in the face of failure, to learn to plan for what to do when failure occurs, and most importantly *to learn from your failures*, just like U.S. Congressman Lewis and the rest of the leaders of the Civil Rights era. Where would we be today if they quit when things got rough?

Every single attempt you make tells you something important. Maybe it tells you something that you need to learn about, or a skill you need to practice. Maybe it tells you about somebody you need to get on your side, or that you simply need more people.

In every situation, the high-performer asks his- or herself: "What went right? What went wrong?" There's a little bit of both in every situation, and you can and *must* learn from both.

Daymond John is a member of the cast of Shark Tank. If you haven't seen it before, it's a show where people with business ideas pitch their ideas to successful entrepreneurs (Sharks), who critique them. Then, the Sharks decide whether to invest in their ideas.

When his wife asked him why he was smiling while one of his businesses stood on the verge of collapse, John told her this:

"Failure is a necessary process."

He knew that every business decision he made was a risk. He knew that he would lose some gambles. When you're operating at his level, you can lose hundreds of thousands of dollars in a single mistaken decision, maybe even millions!

But John knew that there was only one way to avoid making mistaken decisions – and that was to simply never make *any decisions at all*. He knew that failing many times over was part and parcel to success.

Every time you fail, if you learn from your failure, that failure makes you better. Some entrepreneurs and CEOs will even refer to failures as "an exciting opportunity." Why? It's an opportunity to learn. An opportunity to grow.

Of course, we must be mindful of our cost-benefit analysis. That's what makes all great leaders great. They ask themselves how much they can afford to risk and they look at the potential consequences. If everything checks out, they risk it. They ask themselves which goals are most powerful and worthy – and those areas are *where* they put their actions where their mouth is and risk failure.

Fail fast, and fail cheaply.

No less a leader than Winston Churchill once defined success as: "The ability to move from failure to failure without losing enthusiasm.

Those who treat failure positively control their own destiny. They are the ones who are able to learn, grow, and ultimately make change.

Those who are too afraid to fail are the ones who, in the ultimate irony, *fail* to make any change because they've failed to take any risks.

We need to become a community of change-makers. And when we do it together, we can lift each other up when we fall.

#7 – *Learn Relentlessly*

There's a mindset in our society that you go to school to learn. Once you're done with school, the theory goes, you're supposed to have all the skills you need for life and you don't need to learn anymore.

That is completely backward.

As we've covered here, schools don't even teach many of the most important life skills. Did you ever take a class on business skills? Maybe a few of you have, if you had a very good school. But most of us haven't.

Did you ever take a class on social skills? A class on community organizing? A class on your local laws and ordinances? A class on political theory? How about a class on obtaining and maintaining excellent credit? A class on building wealth? A class on entrepreneurship?

Most of us have never taken classes on those subjects. So it's up to us to do the research ourselves. If we don't learn new skills and more information, we can't grow as people or as change-makers.

The good news is, we live in the information age. There's almost nothing we *can't* learn about on the Internet if we take the time and energy to do so.

The next part of learning is a little trickier: actually implementing those skills in our lives, and acting on the new knowledge we've gained. This is where we risk failing and making mistakes. It can be uncomfortable. But as we've already seen above, failing and making mistakes are also completely necessary for our growth – and our success.

As you push yourself to research, learn, practice, and take risks, you might be surprised how fast you begin to see change in your own life. Your newfound confidence from your small wins will shore up your confidence and enthusiasm in your mission.

This, then, becomes a happy feedback cycle. The more you learn, the more you *want* to learn.

#8 – *Celebrate Your Successes*

No one else is you. And that's your power. If you don't believe in yourself, who will? Confidence is contagious. People want to be around those who exude confidence and a sense of purpose.

Always remember: we never WIN or LOSE. We WIN or we LEARN.

When you fail, learn the lesson. Then you've succeeded.

And most of all, *celebrate* those successes. Even if it's just learning from a failure, honor and recognize yourself when you do something that you've never done before.

The mind is powerful. It determines everything that we do. And it believes what you feed it.

If you feed your mind a steady diet of celebration of success, your mind will understand that you *are* a success. And that will make it easy to stay excited about bigger and better wins for all of us.

#9 – *Master Your Mind*

If you don't master your mind, your mind will master you. A mind that is not cultivated to create the mindset of success will instead be dominated by the prevailing culture. We can't let this happen. Our culture is not one that wants us to create real and lasting change. We cannot leave our mind at its disposal.

An uncultivated mind sabotages your purpose, your business, your finances, your family, and your community. It second-guesses you and tells you not to rock the boat. Not to take risks. Not to try and risk failure.

Cultivate your mind to focus on what you want with great positivity. With exercises like those we've discussed above, we can shape our mind into anything we want it to be.

To achieve lasting change, it is essential to avoid the ***three Ds***:

Doubting – Doubting whether you should move forward. Doubting whether you should learn. Doubting whether you should work together. Doubting whether you should try.

Disbelieving – Believing that a better world is not possible or is not worth it, so there's no point in trying. This is a terrible place to be, and all too easy to fall into if we listen to the messages of the culture around us instead of consciously shaping our own beliefs.

Diminishment – In diminishment, you are seeing results from your actions – but doubt and disbelief set in anyway. You begin to diminish the results you're seeing, and tell yourself they're so small, they don't really matter. In a mindset of diminishment, no result is enough to justify the effort. So the effort soon stops happening.

To assist you in mastering your mind, practice visualization, box breathing, and affirmations every day. Surround yourself with positive, like-minded people.

Success is supposed to be fun and enjoyable – and it can be, when it's shared.

Believe and you *will* achieve. We will all achieve a better world for our children.

#10 – Set the Right Expectations

We've already discussed the importance of failure to learning and growth. I want to emphasize this again, because it's so important.

So many people give up because their work is not an overnight success, or because they make a mistake. Yet real, lasting change only comes from *consistent* work – work that persists despite failures and mistakes.

You must expect mistakes and failure. You cannot expect overnight success. Reach for the impossible – but recognize that it will take years or even decades to get there. If the great Civil Rights leaders of the past had given up when they didn't reach their goal within a few months or years – well then, there wouldn't have *been* any Civil Rights movement.

This isn't about reigning in your ambition. "Unrealistic" expectations are good. But they must be paired with patience, if the "unrealistic" is to become reality.

If you don't hit a home run the first time you pick up a baseball bat and that discourages you, you'll never learn to play baseball. Remember: just one home run can change your life, and every attempt is another chance.

So reach for the stars. But know that to get there, you'll have to be in it for the long haul.

#11 – Trust What You Know

Trusting in what we know gives us the courage to try new things. Whether it's a firm sense of right and wrong, faith in God, a vision of a better future, or faith in yourself, being grounded in a firm base that we *know is correct* and which *drives our every action* is a ticket to success.

Here are some things I know that I'd like to share with you:

1. God is faithful. If you trust Him you cannot fail. This is why I believe I cannot lose. This is why I trust that every failure is a lesson we will need later for greater success.

2. The Sun will rise tomorrow. Nothing is the end of the world. This has been true for billions of years. The Sun always rises tomorrow, and life goes on. Nothing can take that away.

3. What you are going through right now will pass. It might take a day, a month, a year. All things change. You can outlast the worst of trials just by growing and continuing to move forward. You typically can't beat the man or woman who

doesn't quit.

4. Be kind, because everyone is going through something. We all experience sadness and frustration, and it can be tempting to take them out on others. But we must understand that mistakes happen. Other people are going through things in life that we can't even imagine.

5. The best things in life aren't things. Growing up poor, this took me a while to realize. The best things in life are not cars, houses, clothes, or jewelry. What's far more valuable than all of those things? Faith. Family. Relationships. Community. Purpose.

   Invest your time in *those* and they will serve you in ways you never dreamed possible.

6. What you get out of life is what you put into it. This means that an average person's level of effort is never going to yield extraordinary rewards.

   If we want to see change in the world, we have to *make* change in the world. This requires extraordinary effort, but it yields extraordinary rewards.

   If you expect more out of life than you put into it, you will be disappointed. If you expect less out of life than you put into it, you'll be pleasantly surprised.

7. Gratitude is the healthiest emotion. You can be thankful for everything around you. Some might say this discourages ambition, but I disagree. We can do far more when we recognize everything we have been given for the gift that it

really is.

Gratitude is better than gratification. Being thankful for what you have feels better than desiring something new. Choose gratitude over gratification every time, and you will have a solid base from which to work wonders.

8. What you focus on becomes your reality. This is true whether you focus on the good or the bad, the possibilities or the impossibilities. It's true whether you focus on lies or truth.

   The future you imagine is the future you are likely to get, especially if you act based on those expectations. So choose your future wisely.

#12 – Your Quality of Life Depends on Your Emotions

Too often we get caught up in feeling that we need a certain level of material comfort, financial success, or social media followers to be content. We measure our success based on these fleeting numbers, which don't translate into lasting transformational change.

If you don't control your thoughts and emotions, your thoughts and emotions will control you. It is important to do things; read things, listen to things, and say things that keep your thoughts and emotions in check.

The quality of your life does not depend on any external factor. It depends on your emotions. In just the same way that *you* are your best investment, your emotions are one of the best investments you can make.

When your emotions are right, everything else will follow.

#13 – *Bitterness Hurts*

Remember that part where what you focus on becomes your reality? Focusing on how you've been wronged or how bad things are won't make things better. If anything, it will degrade your hope, feed your doubts, and diminish your view of your own achievements. We already know what that is, don't we? A recipe for failure. Anger is a powerful thing. It can be a powerful force for good. But know when to draw the line between the anger that motivates and changes your behavior for the better, and the anger that *de*-motivates.

#14 – *The Only Difference Between a Rut and a Grave*

You know how we say we're "stuck in a rut" when we're doing the same things over and over, and we're not seeing any progress toward our goals? It's an easy thing to become stuck in a rut, especially in a society that *prefers* we do the same thing over and over, instead of trying something new.

What's a rut? It's a hole in the ground that you can't get out of. What's a grave? The same thing.

The only difference between a rut and a grave is how long you stay in it.

So make sure you're always moving forward. Only by growing and evolving ourselves will we ever create a flourishing and evolved world.

#15 – *Just Do It*

You could spend your whole life planning and not actually *do* anything. On the other hand, you could spend your life stumbling blindly forward with no plan and still end up in a pretty good place.

Research is important. Learning is important. Strategizing is important.

But at the end of the day, these things are *only as important as the actions you take* based on all that prep work.

So do something. Do anything. Climb up out of your rut and do something new. I've already suggested many courses of action you can take to start building a better future for your community throughout this book, and these suggestions are by no means the only ones.

You've got to try things. Don't wait for the perfect opportunity. It will never come, because perfection is an illusion.

Perfection is something we must *act* to create. It's not something that gets dropped in our laps.

Remember, a failure isn't a failure. It's an opportunity to learn and grow.

And just one success will make you believe that you can have success again.

All great successes are made up of a thousand little ones. All impossible changes are made up of several daily changes.

So let's go start working on the "impossible" changes that we want to see. The more little changes we make in our lives, the closer that brighter future will become.

I hope this information is as valuable to your social justice work as it has been to my businesses. I firmly believe that the methods for success are the same in each, even if the goals are different.

So let's get out there and make the change we want to see in the world.

Family. Finance. Culture. Leadership. Electoral politics. Collective Action. Revolutionary changes to our thinking. All of these are necessary to get to where we need to go, even if we never gain the reparations that are justly due to us.

But you know what they say: "many hands make for light work." And we, the Black community have a great many strong hands.

Let's go use them.

About the Author

Reco McDaniel McCambry comes from humble beginnings. He grew up in a single-parent home, spending some time in the housing projects south of Atlanta, Georgia. He credits his mother for providing the foundation for a legacy that many could only dream of.

His first book, "The Fatherless Father," shares his own story and describes a path to success for the fatherless and single mothers dealing with the journey of raising a child alone. It's based on several real-life examples, stories, and a plan that can resonate with and inspire anyone close to the fatherless epidemic.

Reco is also a serial entrepreneur who has founded four multimillion-dollar companies and has been voted among the top 10% of direct-selling CEOs globally. Graduating from Southern Polytechnic State University with a B.S. degree in Industrial Engineering, he also obtained his M.B.A. degree from the Coles College of Business at Kennesaw State University where he earned a 4.0 GPA.

At the time of the last update of this book, Reco serves as the President & CEO of Novae, a national financial services and training company. In addition, recently launching a venture capital, management, and consulting firm called Urban Sharks, focused on the funding and growth of minority owned companies.

He's a member of the Forbes Business Council, the Golden Key International Society, and Beta Gamma Sigma, the #1 business honors society in the world. Recognized for his strong leadership, he also serves on the Leadership Council of the National Small Business Association (NSBA) out of Washington, D.C. In addition to many other honors, he has been recognized multiple times since 2008 in "Who's Who in Black Atlanta," a publication highlighting some of the most accomplished African Americans in and around Atlanta, GA.

Understanding firsthand what it takes to go from the projects to prosperity, Reco has been inspired to offer mentorship in both life and business to as many people as possible. Knowing the value of community, role models, and mentorship, he speaks frequently at nonprofits and youth programs and offers free business mentorship calls for budding entrepreneurs and individuals, in general, that are in search of success in life.

Reco now seeks to use his platform to promote social justice, progress, and true reparations for the Black community, using both the skills of the business world and of community organizing.

For more information on Reco McCambry, please visit:

www.RecoMcCambry.com

Made in the USA
Monee, IL
20 September 2020